ʻNN

ʼRTEZ

# WHY

# MAKE

# EAGLES

# SWIM?

EMBRACING NATURAL STRENGTHS
IN LEADERSHIP & LIFE

GREENLEAF
BOOK GROUP PRESS

Published by Greenleaf Book Group Press
Austin, Texas
www.gbgpress.com

Distributed by Greenleaf Book Group

For ordering information or special discounts for bulk purchases, please contact Greenleaf Book Group at PO Box 91869, Austin, TX 78709, 512.891.6100.

Design and composition by Greenleaf Book Group
Cover design by Greenleaf Book Group
© Richard Lowthian. Used under license from Shutterstock.com
© Javier Brosch. Used under license from Shutterstock.com

Cataloging-in-Publication data is available.

Print ISBN: 978-1-62634-336-8

eBook ISBN: 978-1-62634-337-5

Part of the Tree Neutral[®] program, which offsets the number of trees consumed in the production and printing of this book by taking proactive steps, such as planting trees in direct proportion to the number of trees used: www.treeneutral.com

TreeNeutral®

Printed in the United States of America on acid-free paper

16 17 18 19 20 21   10 9 8 7 6 5 4 3 2 1

First Edition

*This book is a product of my wife's limitless and insightful support. And its concepts have been reinforced and expanded by the lessons our children and grandchildren have taught us day by day. But as much as it's dedicated to my family, it's also dedicated to my clients, colleagues, readers, and all other students of attributes—both current and future. I pray that the truth and tools in these pages will continue to infuse your life, your work, and your relationships with new meaning and power.*

—Bill

# CONTENTS

# INTRODUCTION

What lies behind us and what lies ahead of us are

tiny matters compared to what lies within us.

—Henry S. Haskins

For many years, clients have been urging me to write this book. It's to their credit, and largely in support of them, that a wider audience can now unleash the power of attributes—the power of honing in on our natural gifts, kicking weaknesses to the curb, and managing others to their greatest potential. At its essence, this book is about shifting our focus to individual strengths. It's a change in thinking that not only makes life and work more enjoyable but also helps to produce more successful teams, realize more innovative outcomes, and instill a more driven and loyal culture.

But I'm getting ahead of myself.

## MY ATTRIBUTES VISION FOR YOU

Every important endeavor should start with a picture of the outcome we're hoping to achieve. So let's start by outlining a clear vision of what you will gain from reading *Why Make Eagles Swim?*

- Become familiar with your own attribute profile—the natural, inborn strengths that define much of your personality and that are key to your personal success, as well as the success of your team or organization. This profile is the framework through which you interpret and respond to your world and the people in it. It guides how you think, prioritize, and decide courses of action. And it determines your behavior and your response to the behavior of others.

- Learn that success lies in optimizing what you're naturally best at, rather than struggling to "fix" your most challenging traits.

- Begin tuning your internal antenna into others in a powerful new way, picking up on the constant stream of clues they broadcast to reveal their own attribute profiles—their own unique strengths and challenges.

- Collect an array of practical tools to help you better understand and grow the individuals and teams that you manage or support.

- Gain a heightened appreciation for the rich variety in people around you, no longer avoiding or dreading those who are most different, but rather valuing them for who they are and how you can help one another grow.

As you learn and practice these concepts and tools, you will gain a better understanding of and appreciation for yourself and others. You'll also learn to maximize your potential and theirs—and become a positive catalyst in helping them do the same. Both you and those you influence will see positive change in your personal lives, on your teams, throughout your organizations, and in your families. You'll tap into the full and unimaginable potential of human beings. You'll overcome obstacles, unearth opportunities, and change relationships for the long term.

## WHY THIS IS DIFFERENT

The real-world feedback that I'll share throughout this book only serves to confirm just how powerful and unique these tools are, because most of the enthusiastic revelations I hear come from people who have done assessments galore: personality, aptitude, talent measurement, culture fit, and so on.

I applaud these efforts of self-discovery. In my long executive career, I benefited from most of them. And this attributes concept will augment all such efforts with its own brand of personal motivation and feel-it-in-your-gut truth.

However, there's also a core difference in the attributes approach, and it represents the main reason I went to work on developing these tools twenty-five years ago: We need a perspective on growth and development that's focused on where we *as well as others* are naturally gifted.

There's plenty of stuff out there that hones in on the question of "who am I?" rather than on "how do I tune in to the people around me?" There's also plenty of advice on how to get better at some behavior that a certain author, speaker, or pundit sees as important. But there's not enough talk about leveraging the unique attributes that we're already great at in order to become exceptional—and certainly not enough material exploring the ways we can help others do the same.

## IT'S PEOPLE STUFF

As a leadership coach, I've put on hundreds of attributes seminars, usually to audiences aiming to enhance the teamwork and performance of their business, church, school, etc. In doing so, I've learned that the benefits of this concept prove equally dramatic at work and at home.

Let's take Mark as an example: After putting on an attributes seminar for the CEO's management team at a fitness company, I had dinner with the group to discuss further questions and examples. The whole team was highly animated following our afternoon together, but I noticed that Mark, the VP of sales, remained very quiet, seemingly unengaged.

"Don't be discouraged by Mark," a few attendees offered later. "He's really formal and very quiet—not an enthusiastic type." In light of this, imagine everyone's surprise when Mark arrived late to the next morning's staff meeting, dressed in casual clothes.

"You guys have to try this attributes stuff," he began. "Last night after dinner, I decided to talk to my seventeen-year-old son about it. He and I have been like strangers for three years. I told him the basics of the concept, admitted that I'd realized I'd been lecturing and not listening, and explained that I wanted a chance to change.

"He lit up, read over my profile and the attributes descriptions, and we talked until 4 a.m.! That's more conversation than we've had in total these past three years."

Needless to say, Mark started talking to each of his salespeople in a whole new way from that day forward.

This kind of thing happens all the time. In the midst of a session with a professional team, attendees will make comments like, "Oh my gosh! That's what's going on with my teenager/spouse/sibling." And after many seminars, someone from the audience will call me to explain that they recapped the concept to their spouse, who quickly decided that the couple should both have their profiles done and work through the program together.

In short, this is not just business stuff. It's personal too, because it's people stuff, and people don't confine themselves to the offices of your life. As you read on, you'll start having insights like, "*That* explains why my boss behaves that way" or "Wow, that sounds exactly like my brother" or "Could this explain my customer's resistance?"

It's a concept with endless real-world relevance. In fact, the single most common comment I get during and after an attributes session is this: "When you described X attribute, I thought you were talking directly to me. Like, *how did he know?!*"

## A NOTE ON EXAMPLES AND CONFIDENTIALITY

Since I've already spouted off a few examples, I should take a moment to explain myself: Because stories are such a powerful learning tool, I have included many examples throughout this book. And every single one of these examples is true in its essence and inspired by actual people and real stories.

Out of genuine respect for you, the reader, I wanted these stories to be real. But out of deep and personal respect for my clients, I am extremely protective of their confidentiality and wanted to ensure that all people discussed in examples were completely unrecognizable, hopefully even to themselves.

To achieve both of these objectives, I've taken the following approach:

- Not surprisingly, every name has been changed. But I've also fictionalized all job titles, positions, industries, product mixes, geographic locations, etc., without compromising the sense of context or the lesson each story imparts. In short, I changed every detail that could be changed without affecting the main point of the example.

- Dialog in the stories, while placed in quotation marks, does not represent any person's exact words, but rather the general information or overall message conveyed during the interchange.

- In some cases, I've woven unrelated, individual events into a single parable.

So any perceived similarity to real life is not only unintended but is also more likely a result of the common behaviors and responses of people with similar attribute profiles. In short, I tell stories designed to show the meaning of real-life experiences, but I do it with imagination to avoid identifying or revealing the particulars of anyone I've coached or otherwise known.

## WHY ME?

Before we go down this road together, you might want to know a few things about the guy who's mapping it out. If you're already wondering about me, then you're probably similar to many of the people I coach. They come in skeptical, and when they approach me, they frame it in different ways (depending on their attributes, of course): either the aggressive version, "What makes you so smart?" or the polite version, "How did you come up with this stuff?"

My answer to both is the same: "doing it wrong, admitting it quickly, and figuring out how to improve." And for a forty-five-year career (so far), I've stuck with that program, adding input and insight from coaching hundreds of people for the last twenty-five years.

I joke with my clients that I'm actually thirty-one and have had gray hair and wrinkles cosmetically added to give me an air of wisdom. But in truth, my development of this concept began in 1966, when I started my own business as a college junior, built it through employing commissioned reps, and sold it before I graduated. From that first venture, I learned a lot about risk, spending money too fast, and winning by helping others win.

After grad school, I taught at the university level for two years, and I realized that I loved teaching. Later, I would discover that this was at the core of my life's purpose. But first, I entered a large corporation and worked my way up through several departments, eventually serving as an officer and general manager of the smallest but most profitable division.

Since we were relatively little and financially healthy, headquarters left us alone. So we had the freedom to try out different people- and team-management approaches. Many worked, some exceedingly well. And through it all, I never stopped trying out different tactics, learning, and improving.

In 1990, I was forty-five and still in love with my job. But I also yearned to try out these management ideas and tools on a larger scale. Plus, my personal vision work had revealed that my true core purpose was teaching. So we launched Bill Munn Management Coaching.

Since then, I've had the satisfaction of watching hundreds of clients apply these principles. And I've learned from every one of them—volumes of insight into how these concepts apply to organizational improvement, leadership development, and personal growth.

Through it all, my extensive corporate experience has proven extremely valuable to my career as a management coach. When I'm working with clients, I'm not just speaking from knowledge I gathered in my MBA studies; I outpaced that information eons ago. I'm speaking from having been where they are, so my empathy is high and my experience essential.

Moreover, these aren't just concepts or academic precepts. They're tools I've personally applied and tested. And time and again, clients tell me that it's a very different experience to walk through this stuff with someone who's been in their shoes.

Today, even after two and a half decades, I'm still gratified when I hear a story about how this approach has helped repair a relationship, get a team to start clicking, mend communication with a teenager, close a customer, fill a job gap with exactly the right candidate, you name it. Somehow, it still amazes me.

So it's a humbling honor that you give your time to this.

Let's dig in.

# PART I

# WHAT'S AN ATTRIBUTE?

# CHAPTER 1

# TRUE TO FORM

This above all; to thine own self be true.

—William Shakespeare

If we'd met him as a child, what might you or I have thought of little Al, the dreamer? A thoughtful kid and reluctant talker who used to repeat sentences quietly to himself, Al was viewed by many as somewhat dull. He didn't conform well to the structure and discipline of primary school; struggled with the quick, automatic responses prized in this educational atmosphere; and never excelled in memorizing words, texts, and names, so his teachers considered him only moderately talented. One particularly harsh Greek teacher predicted that

Al would never get anywhere. And he did in fact fail the entrance exam at the polytechnic institute where he aimed to study.

Those dearest to him recognized his differences as well: Al's sister and closest friend described him as calm, dreamy, and slow—although at once self-assured and determined. And his own parents were so concerned about Al's slow progress with language that they consulted a doctor on the matter. But his mother was ambitious and encouraged her son's self-reliance, and his father provided a sound counterbalance of a comforting, supportive environment where Al could develop his own personality.[1]

So what happened to him? Little Albert Einstein grew up to be a giant in the field of physics. Although he never excelled in basic math, his creative imagination was the natural strength that allowed him to make great scientific leaps, like recognizing that light waves must bend as they pass a planet's gravitational field. A key to Einstein's success was the fact that he learned to accept and leverage the unstructured way his mind worked. For example, when he was stumped while working on a complex math problem, he formed the habit of leaving the blackboard and playing his violin. Many times, the solution came to him in the midst of making music.

• • •

And speaking of making things, let's look at Steve. Exacting Steve, who was such an extreme perfectionist that he lived without furniture because nothing he found was just right. As a boss, he was demanding, a micromanager so goal driven that he showed virtually zero empathy toward people. In his determined pursuit of perfection, Steve was often abrasive toward his team, who grumbled that his goals and deadlines were completely unrealistic.

But, as it turned out, they were not impossible. Steve's driven perfectionism led his company to widely acclaimed excellence in product design and development. His blindness to others' feelings kept him ruthlessly focused on priorities. And his exacting deadlines and micromanagement yielded unimaginable feats of innovation.

He was Steve Jobs, founder and former CEO of Apple. And, although he admitted that his strongest attributes were sometimes his shortcomings as a leader, he also lived according to his strengths, leveraging his gifts into a groundbreaking agile empire that reimagined and permanently altered numerous industries, including personal computing, music, film, retailing, and more.[2]

· · ·

But no one personifies innovation like Tom. Young Tom's teacher described him as mentally confused and muddled; overall, her assessment would probably equate to extreme attention deficit disorder in today's terms. He was so disruptive in class that he was expelled after a total of three months of schooling. But his expulsion led his mother to homeschool her son, and Tom later credited his success to this education, since she gave him the freedom to exert his creativity.

Throughout his adult life, Tom continued to resist structure and large organizations, and he remained very disorganized. For example, after one of his laboratories burned down, he remembered that he'd failed to purchase fire insurance. But despite his challenges, Tom let his creative side soar.

The result? Thomas Edison became a hugely successful inventor, accumulating over 2,300 patents worldwide. His innovations include the phonograph, the movie camera, and a storage battery for an electric car—in addition to a little gadget known as the electric light bulb.[3]

## SEEDS OF A GIFT

Would you plant an apple seed and try to nurture it into an orange tree? No matter what type of fertilizer you used, no matter how carefully you monitored the water and sun, you would never succeed in making that apple seed bear oranges. (Although you may interfere with its ability to produce great apples.)

Human beings are like this. We each have seeds for different types of fruit in us, but too often, we spend our lives trying to become something we're not—in part because we take our natural gifts for granted, and in part because we spend so much time focusing on what we're *not* good at that we lose sight of the ways we're great.

Albert Einstein, Steve Jobs, and Thomas Edison were each built to bear a certain type of fruit, and they didn't waste their energy trying to become something else. Instead, they unapologetically functioned according to their strengths—they focused on augmenting their natural gifts. And they changed the world.

So can you.

Here's some news that shouldn't be news at all: You're better than you think you are. So is your team. So are those people in your family you're always harping on. But instead of *being* better, you're spending too much time trying to be—well, something else. Something you're not built for. Some version of *you* that you think you're supposed to be, rather than the best *you* for which you're already designed.

Fortunately, you can change this. You can learn and practice tools that nurture your strongest traits—what we'll refer to as power-alley attributes. As you do this, you'll ditch unproductive habits and constructs, and you'll experience what your personal best really feels like.

## THE EAGLE AND THE LOON

My wife and I live on a lake where we're blessed to see beautiful wildlife in our front yard every day: deer and rabbit, mink and fox, herons, loons, and even bald eagles. What a breathtaking sight those eagles are—so grand in scale, so powerful in the air.

But what if I told you that every day an eagle walked out to the end of our dock, tiptoed hesitantly to the edge, and spent the morning doing nosedives into the calm water, trying to improve his swimming skills? Turns out, as he's soaring over our northern lakes at a thousand feet of altitude, using his remarkably sharp eyes to scan the water for shallow-swimming fish, he keeps seeing loons working below him, and he's amazed by their skill in the water.

For those of you less familiar with the North Country, loons are a symbol of pristine northern wilderness lakes, and they are fascinating creatures. You may have heard a recording of their haunting song, which is sure to crop up in any film where a Walden-like lakeside retreat comes into play. But many people don't know that unlike most flying birds, loons have solid bones that help them dive to depths of up to two hundred feet. The extra weight makes it difficult for them to take off in flight, but it also makes them incredible deep-water fishers.

Impressive, right? That's what the eagle thinks. So now, he's spending his days on the end of our dock instead of up in the sky. He's lamenting his shallow dives, groaning because he doesn't have those red eyes designed to scan the lake's darkest depths, and complaining about his underwater lung capacity.

But when the eagle's out soaring on his fishing rounds, the loon's entire family is looking up at him, talking about how great it would be if their loon boy could fly that way. He could hunt the whole lake in a few minutes, swoop down suddenly, surprise his prey, and be gone in seconds, avoiding competitors. Clearly, that eagle has a good thing going. Why doesn't the loon learn those traits?

This whole thing sounds crazy, right? So here's my question: Why are we all spending so much time trying to make eagles swim? Why don't we put more energy into the ways we're naturally built to be great?

Here's what I think is crazy: sitting down with a top salesperson for a performance review, only to spend eighty percent of that time discussing how she might improve the accuracy of the expense reports she's forever struggling with. That's eighty percent of a meeting spent telling an eagle to work on her backstroke—to take time away from flying in favor of fumbling around in the water. Meanwhile, elsewhere in the organization, someone's asking a gifted administrator to focus on improving his big-picture thinking. And someone else is (yet again) chastising a standout creative on the product-development team for his struggle with follow-through.

What is going on here? Why are we spending so much time focusing on weaknesses and so little time discussing how to leverage those natural strengths? Instead, let's get the eagle back in the air and the loon focused on deep dives. Encourage the exemplary salesperson to close her computer, get face-to-face with prospects, and exceed her new target; invite the detailed administrator to help with those expense reports; and put the creative person in a brainstorming room to focus on imagining the next great innovation worth selling in the first place. Suddenly, everyone wins. Sales are stellar, expenses are accurate and timely, and the company is working on some breakthrough new products.

That's the power of attributes.

Now listen: Eagles actually *can* swim when they need to. But their competence in the water is nothing like their expertise in the air. And loons *can* fly, but they need up to a quarter mile of water-surface runway to get all that weight in the air. It's deep diving where they blow the competition away, so that's what they should (and do) expend the most time and energy on.

We too can fly higher and dive deeper by focusing our energy on the unique talents intrinsic to each of us. These are our natural attributes. Most great success stories start with this approach.

## WHAT'S AN ATTRIBUTE? (AND WHAT ISN'T?)

An attribute is an inherent trait. It's a natural characteristic that can greatly influence your perception of and behavior toward the world around you. Think of your attribute profile as the way you're wired—the built-in programming of your own internal microchip.

If we were studying physical attributes, we might look at height, eye color, gender, etc.—things that are easy to see. Such traits affect how we perceive and interact with the world around us. For example, a friend of mine had a son who was six feet eleven inches tall and played in the NBA. When he walked through a house, he ducked at each doorway. But when I asked him about it, he wasn't even aware of ducking. For him, it was instinctive—like blinking. Back when he was first outgrowing doorframes, he'd only had to hit his head on a few before he learned. The height attribute led to a behavior modification.

The nonphysical attributes we're studying here can (and usually do) lead to the same thing. Although more hidden from view, these attributes are very real qualities of who we are—at least as definitive, and certainly much more important, than the color of our eyes. Let's look at Lauren, who has a huge dose of empathy (sharing other peoples' emotions). When talking to someone who has just heard sad news, Lauren's face looks much like that of the person speaking. Tears come. She can feel the other person's pain. She cares, and she hurts. This response is real and natural—like blinking. It's an automatic, reflexive reaction. That's an attribute.

And therein lies our essential success secret. According to Lewis Schiff, author of *Business Brilliant: Surprising Lessons from the Greatest Self-Made Business Icons* (New York: HarperBusiness, 2013), "nearly sixty percent of middle-class people strive to get better at tasks they are not good at. Exactly zero percent of high net worth individuals [say] the same."[4] Of course, I'm not implying that net worth is everyone's ultimate measure of success; your own unique life vision will determine your goals. But since high net worth often reflects a successful career, it's worth noting that this group claims to invest no time at all in improving on so-called weaknesses.

Just think how often you hear caveats when learning about highly successful people. Walt Disney was a creative visionary whose legendary ideas changed the entertainment industry forever, *but* he was a completely incompetent artist who couldn't draw Mickey Mouse if asked.[5] John Adams served on more committees in the Continental Congress than any other individual and played a huge role in bringing the United States into existence as a nation, *but* he was only a mediocre speaker, tended to take offense easily, and was generally regarded as vain.[6]

The "but" is always there—for every person. Yet for those who become great, it's a side note to the real story. We don't remember Walt Disney as a poor artist; we remember him as a visionary genius. We don't look back on John Adams as a touchy guy; we recognize him as a man who helped mold the US democratic system. We remember great men and women for the strengths that they leveraged, not the weaknesses they improved upon.

What if Walt had spent his life trying to figure out how to draw that mouse? What a sad prospect. Yet many of us can imagine how he might have gotten off track in pursuit of such a skill. So let's make sure we understand skills and knowledge as they relate to attributes.

## Attributes versus Skills

Attributes are not the same as skills. A skill is something you learn to do. It's not instinctive. Skills include driving a car, brain surgery, and carpentry.

Although an attribute may enhance your success at learning a skill, the skill itself is not an attribute. For example, someone who has a strong communication-related attribute can likely get his point across clearly to others and hold an audience's attention during his explanation. To further leverage this trait, he might hone the skills of composition, creative writing, or public speaking. But the skills alone do not make an attribute.

## Attributes versus Knowledge

Likewise, attributes are different from knowledge. Knowledge is something you learn, whether or not you end up using it in any way.

If you are a mathematician, chemist, or historian, your chosen specialty is largely based on knowledge. And your success in acquiring knowledge may be enhanced by certain attributes, such as thirst for learning or precision in note-taking. But the knowledge is not the attribute; it's a body of information you've assimilated.

It's worth noting that your attributes can powerfully affect how you use your knowledge. For example, a politician who is strong in the attribute of conceptual thinking might make a concerted effort to study historical facts. Then, he could use his attribute to apply that knowledge, linking patterns of history together to conceptualize a new way of approaching a current societal problem.

Although attributes are not learned the way skills and knowledge are, you can improve upon your attributes by increasing your related knowledge and skills. For example, if you are a natural people person, you can enhance your listening skills and improve your knowledge of human emotion and feeling to help that attribute flourish.

But as we'll discuss, if interaction with people is a huge challenge area for you, it might *not* be worth your time to focus on such skills. Always be prudent. Although this type of training could very well help you in some way, you have a finite and precious amount of time and energy to offer. If you want to live and work at your full potential, please don't waste it. Don't take swimming lessons if you're an eagle. Prioritize your natural gifts, and you'll be amazed at the heights you can reach.

## A LONG ROAD WITH A QUICK START

One final note of encouragement as you begin learning and applying this attributes concept—you will see results quickly. Some things in life take years. Not this.

In the introduction, I told you the story of Mark. He saw results the first night! Like him, you'll probably begin seeing results shortly after you start trying the tools. Usually, this happens within weeks or months. But it's up to you—it's all a matter of when you begin accepting the concept and taking action.

So I encourage you to give it a go. Open your mind. Take notes while you read. Reread. Experiment. Ask for insight and help. Share your insights and questions with others. Do it together, with your team, your family, or your group. Visit www.AttributesAcademy.com for additional tools and tactics. In short, take action.

· · ·

This brings me to the matter of resistance—the idea that we will succeed by focusing on our natural strengths makes good, intuitive sense. And as we've already seen, we're surrounded by examples and evidence that clearly support the power of this approach to life and work. Yet for many of us, it's hard to let go of that nagging urge to focus on our so-called weaknesses.

So it's time to address this important question: If this is such a fruitless approach, how did we get stuck in this rut in the first place? How did this bias toward the negative take hold?

# CHAPTER 2

# OUR NEGATIVE BIAS

Death is not the greatest loss in life. The greatest loss is what dies within us while we live.

—Norman Cousins

Assuming that you have normal color vision, how would you respond if you found out I suffer from colorblindness? Would you blame me for seeing differently than you do? Ridicule me? Of course not. We both know that it's the way I'm built and simply a natural difference between us. If you decide that my colorblindness is a weakness, then I suppose you'd be just as likely to judge me for my height or hair color. But I'm guessing that you'd consider such judgments nonsensical.

Similarly, how do you respond to people who speak a different language than you do? Even if it's difficult (or impossible) for you to understand them, I highly doubt that you assume what they have to say is irrelevant. You simply recognize that some study and patience will be necessary for you to communicate.

Attributes work in the same way. You might see things differently than certain members of your team—or certain members of your family, fraternity, board of elders, you name it. At times, it may even seem like they speak another language. But the differences aren't a matter of good and bad. In fact, they add depth and dimension to our lives.

Our differences are one exciting result of the many inherent traits on display in the human family, and they ultimately add to the rich variety of our world—and provide the basis for our ability to improve, innovate, and grow as individuals and societies. If every person had the same attributes, can you imagine how boring our same-old, been-there world would be? Not to mention how difficult it would be to make changes and grow? To reach new heights, we need different brains working in different ways.

When you start to recognize these nuances—start tuning in to the dynamism of the attribute-filled people around you—a world of new potential will emerge. It's just a matter of understanding the attribute landscape and managing it wisely. Case in point, the color-blindness we discussed earlier. Do you know what color-blind people are terrific at? Spotting enemy positions in war zones, because their eyes aren't fooled by camouflage.

Every attribute has its purpose.

## A PARADIGM SHIFT

The way we judge or value attributes isn't a result of our wiring, but a byproduct of our experiences. Maybe as a kid, you brought home a report card with As in all subjects, but a D in math. Your parents' response? Disappointment over the D, meetings with your math teacher, and new rules and attention around your math homework. Total focus on your "problem" area.

What signal did you get from this parental reaction? Concentrate on what you're bad at. Put the most work into "fixing" the things that come hardest to you. Invest maximum time and effort in working on the negative.

Or maybe you were scolded for exhibiting certain attributes in your younger years: "Why are you always so pushy?" "Stop being so sensitive." "You're bossy!" In fact, these tendencies may have been signs of great traits—potentially strong ingredients in your recipe for future success. But early on, you were conditioned to believe that such behavior wasn't good, and you repressed certain attributes.

That's a hard lesson to forget. But here's the good news: You can unlock them again. Even in adulthood, you can rediscover who you really are and set those great traits free.

Of course, it's not family alone that teaches us how to view others and ourselves. The biases of the world we live in can also confuse our thinking, which you may understand all too well if you've been labeled with one of our culture's insistently negative terms for describing a unique set of gifts and challenges: obsessive-compulsive disorder (every single word has an undesirable connotation);

attention deficit disorder (why frame this as a *deficit of attention* instead of an *abundance of interest*?); or any other learning "disorder." If everything is a disorder, what defines normal?

The fact is, we tend to be callous and flip in our negative depiction of attributes that are different or more extreme than our own. Which leads us to lose sight of the greatness therein. Take the attention deficit disorder (ADD) example: We have a number of ADD people in our family, and I'm pleased to point out that, while they all have their share of challenges (don't we all?), they also enjoy the positives typical of many ADD brains, namely strong creativity, spontaneity, and innovative thinking.

Another example is particularly moving: The parents and caregivers of autistic children have often shared a heartfelt concern for the future careers of their little ones. "How will he make a living? What happens when I'm not here to provide?"

But over the years, research has revealed more and more about the incredible attributes of the autistic mind—chiefly, an off-the-charts ability to see minute detail, recognize how those details tie together in the whole, and create new patterns in bringing it all together.[1] And guess what occupation those traits are perfectly suited to: computer coding. Pretty good job market, folks!

It's time to unlearn some old, ingrained negative biases and relearn (and accept) how to recognize and appreciate your unique and specific set of gifts. Gifts that you can leverage into great advantages for yourself, your team, your family—you name it. To do so, it's helpful to understand where our obsession with weaknesses has come from. Over the years, I've identified three forces that fuel this.

## Force 1: The Myth of Well-Roundedness

The myth of well-roundedness says that life is a quest to get really good at everything. I don't know who started this fantasy, but chasing such a goal means that we focus our attention on a weak trait, "conquer" it, and then turn to the next problem area. In our pursuit of becoming good at everything, we're constantly putting energy toward our deficiencies instead of our strengths.

Here's how it plays out: We start out great at a few things. And since we're already good at this stuff, we say, "Okay, I've got those skills down pat, so there's no need to waste my attention on them. Instead, I'll move on to a skill that I really struggle with and try to overcome my challenges with it." This attitude of trying to be good at everything is like approaching life as if it's a spinning-plates act in a circus: You take a dozen dinner plates and balance each one on a pole by keeping everything spinning at once. To prevent the whole lot from crashing to the floor, you teeter up- and downstage, scrambling to keep the slow-spinning plates moving faster and prevent them from falling.

But what would happen if you let most of the plates drop and instead focused all your energy on two fast-spinning, high-in-the-sky plates? You'd certainly become less frantic. But you'd also spin those strong plates even better. You'd *feel* better. And you'd probably put on a more graceful performance.

I say, let the weak plates drop! Ignore them if you're that brave. Or at minimum, stop *focusing* on them. Because if you try to keep everything spinning, the best case is that you'll succeed in looking like you're just okay at lots of different things. And the worst case is, you'll fumble with everything and drop the whole lot.

At some level, it comes down to choosing the most effective use of your time and energy. It's not that you can't make some improvement in the areas where you struggle most. It's that you have a limited supply of resources to expend, so it's essential to be smart and honest as you prioritize.

People don't succeed in life by pursuing the chimera of well-roundedness. Take George Washington for example: Many historians consider him a rather mediocre military strategist.[2] In fact, Washington disliked battle[3] and was a man of very average intelligence.[4]

So how did he succeed in the Revolutionary War? The credit has gone to his people skills. Washington was great at assembling excellent teams and empowering them to perform. He was gifted at listening, relating to others, and reconciling conflict. He selected highly capable individuals for his cabinet—people who often disagreed with him and one another—and he rarely directed them. Instead, he used patience, persuasion, and his immense personal charisma and credibility to accomplish results. And speaking of results, he's been ranked as one of the three best presidents of the United States.[5]

Again and again, we find that such high-achieving individuals have significant shortcomings—often a backpack full of them. We've now looked at examples like Albert Einstein, Steve Jobs, Walt Disney,

George Washington—we could continue indefinitely. Each one had his not-so-hot traits. But these people didn't focus on so-called weaknesses. Instead, they achieved success by optimizing their strongest attributes—and often ignoring the rest. So history doesn't call them well-rounded. History calls them great.

Effectiveness is not just about whether something *can* be done. It's about what could have been done with the same expenditure of time and effort. But if you still struggle to believe that well-roundedness is a myth, take this three-step challenge:

1. Write out your own definition of "success."

2. List a few relatable people in history—say, from the past five hundred years—who you think meet your definition of success.

3. Read a complete biography of each person on your list.

After that study, send me the name of a "well-rounded" person you've discovered. Just one. I have presented this challenge in hundreds of attributes seminars, and in twenty-five years of presentations, I've never received a name.

Having read extensive historical and biographical accounts myself, I couldn't submit a name either.

## Force 2: Taking Gifts for Granted

It may surprise you to learn that your attribute profile began to form very early in life—probably as soon as age five, and certainly by the time you were ten. In fact, the longer I work with the attributes concept, the more evidence I collect on how early these traits show up. For example, I have kept notes on each of my ten grandchildren since they were toddlers. Several of them are now teenagers whose attributes are more evident and ingrained, and when I review the notes I took when they were small, I find that little has changed.

By the time you were the age of these teenagers, you were already accustomed to your attributes, just as you were accustomed to breathing, blinking, and swallowing. Similar to these reflexive physical actions, exhibiting your attributes became largely automatic for you. Maybe you naturally felt the hurt or joy that your friends were feeling. Or you were driven to achieve, measuring performance by racing against a stopwatch or comparing your grades from quarter to quarter. Or perhaps you sought order and structure, lining up toys in careful rows, straightening crooked pictures on the wall, and correcting typos as you started reading the newspaper. These were all early (and lifelong) signs of your inherent attributes.

Two of my own daughters showed us a great example of attributes appearing early in life: When they played dolls together as girls, my youngest would always verbalize a running story, creating scenes and characters and dialog. Frustrated, she often complained that her sister never *said* anything.

"You have to have a story," the little Communicator would lament. But my eldest had no interest in the story. Instead, she was laser focused on arranging doll furniture, designing home layouts with blocks, and setting up rooms in the dollhouse. Twenty-five years later, my youngest daughter is a writer, and my oldest daughter is an interior designer and shop owner.

Later on, we'll talk further about exploring your own youth for hints of attributes. But for now, just take one point to heart: Your longtime familiarity with your own gifted areas can lead you to write off your most powerful traits. By adulthood, many of us have buried our best attributes under so many layers that we don't even know they're there. Or we don't value them at all: "Sure, I'm organized. But everyone can be organized. And anyway, it's not important. What's important is how driven you are."

But when it comes to attributes, thinking in terms of "important" or "unimportant" means we're missing the point entirely. (In fact, if you decide that attribute X is good and attribute Y is bad, try to remember that if attribute X were in your power alley, you'd suddenly be tuned in to its *dis*advantages.) It's all a matter of conditioning.

I see this with clients all the time. I'll notice a strong attribute and say something like, "You're very good at recognizing cause and effect. Let's work from that trait and optimize it." And my client will immediately respond by explaining that this ability is no big deal—that it's very common. People often say, "Sure, but *everyone* does that."

No. Everyone does *not* do that. I guarantee that whatever your strongest attributes are, I work with people who struggle with those very same traits—and who take your greatest challenge areas for granted. I'd like you all to meet one another and exchange notes.

But since we're not sitting down together today, let's look at an example that we all know: Mother Teresa. She ministered and cared for some of the sickliest and most shunned people of India. When interviewers expressed amazement that she could risk her life among contagious people, she expressed amazement at their surprise.

"Intense love does not measure, it just gives,"[6] she said. With her strong caregiver nature, she didn't think about caring for people, or about why she did it. She just cared. To her, it was not a big deal.

## Force 3: The Desire to Help

From our formative years, those who love us often push their own paradigms on us, encouraging us to pursue that which they believe will help us most in life. The disorganized father thinks that his lack of order held him back, so he pushes his kids to get organized. The extrovert aunt succeeds in sales, and then pressures her relatively introverted nephew to be more outgoing so he might follow in her footsteps. The mentor who loses his job in two consecutive mergers influences his pupil to become a lawyer for perceived job security and income potential.

Although the intention behind such efforts is good, the outcome is often harmful and results in getting others focused on areas where they might not naturally excel. The young people in these examples may well exhibit attributes at odds with their elders' experience, so they will struggle to become average salespeople or lawyers rather than excellent creative directors or psychologists.

We should also watch out for the destructive tendency that demeans a young person's dreams with so-called logic: "You can't make a living doing *that*." What a way to squelch a young artist's creativity or discourage the risk-taking tendency of a great adventurer. If you heard such advice as a young person, know that a huge number of entrepreneurs, writers, artists, inventors, and other groundbreakers ignored the voices that advised them to take a "safer" path.

This is what I call "you ought to" advice, and it is often a dangerous trap. Here's how it works: Pete says you ought to be a teacher. Is this because Pete thinks you have a teacher's attribute profile? Rarely. More often, it's because he wishes he had long summer breaks or a more secure job. When Nancy suggests that you ought to try nursing, is it because she sees caring and people-centric traits in you? Or is it because she'd like to make a nurse's salary herself?

When people give you "you ought to" advice, try asking them about what attributes they see in you to support their suggestion. If they pause and stare blankly, it's probably a sign that they're seeing *your* path through the lens of *their* goals.

Let's look at a historical example of this: Anna Mary Robertson was a farmer's wife who helped support the family by doing needlework for local customers. But arthritis closed that door in 1938, when she was seventy-five years old. Friends and family reminded her that she *ought to* retire anyway. But instead, she began expressing her artistic attribute through painting. When the local drugstore displayed one of her pieces, a collector happened by, bought it, and displayed it in New York City. By age 101, Anna Mary Robertson had completed sixteen hundred more works as the artist Grandma Moses.[7]

Coaching people of all ages has taught me many great lessons, and one of the most consistent truths is this: The vast majority of people who give career advice have themselves spent much of their career in a job they consider mediocre—or downright awful. And in most every case, it's because they have never pursued their strongest attributes. Sadder still, they've probably never understood their own attributes to begin with.

• • •

Let's make sure we understand ours, beginning with a solid starter list of traits.

# CHAPTER 3

# ATTRIBUTE INVENTORY

*What you are is God's gift to you; what you become is your gift to God.*

—Hans Urs von Balthasar

To further illustrate the concept of attributes and to define a shared language we can refer to throughout this book, let's establish a basic list of common traits. I have used these terms and definitions with many client teams over the years, and the list has proven to be a good representation. But before you take a look, please keep three caveats in mind:

1. **Beware of categorizing each attribute as good or bad.** There are no positive or negative attributes—just different ones, each

with its own advantages and disadvantages. (Remember our colorblindness example?) Unlocking the potential of all that variety is a key force for growth within teams.

2.  **As you study the list, watch for your emotional response to certain terms.** While every word has a common denotation—its dictionary definition—the connotative meaning can vary widely. We each have unique emotional responses to certain words, and my chosen vocabulary may not always work for you. For example, if I use the word "father" with an audience, the term will conjure up loving feelings of security for some folks, and feelings of judgment, disappointment, or loss for others. If a name rubs you the wrong way, simply change the word you use. Just be sure to keep your definitions consistent for you and your team.

3.  **Finally, note that this is not a complete catalog of attributes.** It's simply a starter list to help you get going. In fact, my complete inventory contains about eighty attributes, and I haven't met everyone in the world yet! To get to fourteen, I eliminated some and folded others into larger, summary characteristics. And I chose the "finalists," which we'll discuss in depth here, using observations of which attributes seem most relevant in organizational team behaviors. I did this not to limit us, but to create a more manageable primer for people

who are new to the concept and to give us a working list for the purposes of this book.

## ACHIEVER

Achievers are accomplishment oriented, and they have a strong tendency to measure. They love to keep score—not to beat someone else, but to track their own progress. If an Achiever enjoys running for exercise, she's likely to record her times and distances. If she has driven the same route to work for years, she probably still times herself. When you show her a tall building, she asks if it's the tallest. Seat her in a sports car, and she'll ask how fast it goes.

If you have high Achievers working with you, you almost don't need to set goals, because they do it themselves. And if they get close to their goals, they raise them on their own, without the boss's direction. It's all about an internal scorecard.

### Clues

- Asks "How much?" "How big?" "What's the record?" "How fast will it go?"

- Compliments managers with phrases like "You never accepted mediocrity" and "You challenged me to be my best."

## Cautions and Tips

An Achiever needs to be reminded to stop and celebrate success along the way, because this doesn't naturally occur to her. The minute she achieves a goal, she raises the bar. But those around her might be motivated by pausing to recognize the accomplishment.

In managing Achievers, keep in mind that their idea of a great boss (or teacher, coach, and so on) is one who raises the bar continuously. They respond very well to encouragement like, "You can do it. You're better than you think you are."

Note that it's easy for folks to misunderstand an Achiever's tendency toward measuring and comparing. One night, I watched a high Achiever friend arrive at a person's home for a party, walk in the front door, and exclaim, "Wow! Beautiful home. How many square feet is it?"

I knew the hostess well and could read the assumptions behind her shocked expression. But in this case, I also knew the Achiever well and am certain that he couldn't care less about the size of his home compared to hers. He's simply a measurer, and he was genuinely interested in the square footage because of that fascination. Now, when a high Commander (discussed later) is also a high Achiever, his motive in asking such questions is likely competitive. But on its own, the Achiever attribute is about internal measurement—not external competition.

## Example

Six-time Olympic medalist Jackie Joyner-Kersee shows many characteristics of the Achiever. As an athlete, she raised the bar constantly (both figuratively and literally, as a high jumper). She selected—and married—a coach who continuously pushed her to achieve more.[1] And she always seemed very focused on her own scorecard rather than on comparing herself to others, explaining that if she studied past champions, it was never to follow them, but to understand what *makes* a champion. In interview after interview, her drive to push on and improve comes through loud and clear. "Every time I lost," she once explained, "it made me more determined to come back because I was never satisfied."[2]

## COMMANDER

Most people are motivated by recognition; Commanders are simply motivated a lot more by it. They pursue fame and adulation. They want acknowledgment, seek the spotlight, and desire high stature and significance in the eyes of others. Commanders seek positions of authority. They want to be in charge of affecting outcomes.

## Clues

- Makes comments like "Did you see what I did?" and "But I did great, too."

- When watching someone get recognized for performance, privately pictures himself getting that public praise (private praise is good, but not good enough).

- Frequently uses the words "I" and "me."

## Cautions and Tips

In leading Commanders, monitor when their drive for power stops contributing and starts hindering performance. Note that others can get very judgmental about this attribute. But a leader's job is not to judge; it's to optimize performance. Commanders can produce standout results by creating clear direction and setting high standards, but they should be cautious of taking over, and they need ongoing reminders that making others feel important is key to success.

## Example

General Patton showed the strength and weakness of the Commander attribute during World War II. He was a powerful and positive leader in a horrendously tough environment, and he could describe the vision to his soldiers in simple, high-clarity terms. And so he achieved results on the battlefield. But in the politically sensitive negotiations that followed victory, Patton failed at diplomacy, causing a firestorm when he tactlessly told the Russians that they would be at war with the United States in a few years.[3]

## COMMUNICATOR

Communicators are naturally great at getting their point across. People understand them. When a Communicator explains something or tells a story, the audience "gets it." Communicators tend to teach and explain, and they want to be sure that their audience understands—that the communication is effective. They respond to conflict by getting parties to talk to one another. Keep in mind that written communication and oral communication are separate attributes, which I've combined in this definition. But they are, in fact, quite different in action. Great writers are often poor speakers and vice versa.

### Clues

- Begins sentences with phrases like "Let me describe" or "I wrote to you explaining . . ."
- Checks for clarity using phrases like "Does that make sense to you?"
- Gets people together for meetings.
- Addresses confusion or misunderstanding by suggesting that parties talk or discuss matters further.

### Cautions and Tips

Communicators need to avoid holding too-long meetings. And since they default to outgoing words, they should beware of poor listening and verboseness. With a concise approach, Communicators can be extremely motivating, but their tendency to use too many words can lose an audience—particularly in public speaking, when less is often more and "talkers" risk diluting the impact of a powerful story or quotation. It's also important for Communicators to understand that others don't tend to share their love of words, so simple vocabulary is best.

## Example

American politician Joe Biden behaves like a high Communicator, judging by his success in explaining complex international issues and his tendency to use many words. He also exhibits a clear desire that the audience understand his point. Parodies of Mr. Biden often poke fun at his stumbling over words. But listen carefully; most often, he stumbled because he kept talking when silence would have had a higher impact.

## CONCEPTUAL

Conceptuals see the forest and completely skip over the trees. They tend to have a vision and hold a big-picture view. When listening to others describing specifics, the Conceptual's mind automatically finds patterns, recognizing common threads among bits of information and jumping quickly from particulars to the overall strategy. Conceptuals often feel bogged down or bored with details. Although they see alternative avenues to explore, they often lose patience with the individual steps involved in pursuing each option to its end.

## Clues

- Resists detailed explanations of problems and plans, preferring brevity, short action lists, and summaries.

- Does not micromanage people, but spends time ensuring that the team is focused on the same vision and leaves the details of implementation in others' hands.

- Says or thinks things like "Don't get bogged down" or "Please envision this" or "Think of where this could lead" or "What's the endgame?"

## Cautions and Tips

Conceptuals need to be cautious of discounting or ignoring people who are high in the Orderly attribute (discussed later). The fine points Orderlies focus on might seem like frustrating minutiae, but it's these very details that can trip up a Conceptual on the way to big vision and grand strategy. Rather than shrugging off detail, a Conceptual can show respect for the Orderly's focus on specifics by making it clear that all help is welcome when it comes to detail and implementation. Admitting weaknesses can motivate others to step up with support.

## Example

Warren Buffett appears to be a Conceptual. When asked his reasons for investing in some huge company, his answer will touch on just one or two essential points. Or, when asked to comment on an enormously complex issue like our tax code, he answers, with great simplicity, that he shouldn't pay a lower rate than his secretary.[4]

Additionally, Buffett has surprised many analytical investors by saying that he has no interest in daily stock market updates and would be happy to receive market data from *The Wall Street Journal* only once a year![5] That's quite a statement from a man who has billions invested. But he's showing his tendency to look at the big picture and avoid detail when it's not absolutely necessary.

## CREATOR

The Creator acts on new ideas. When shown a fresh concept, she quickly moves to "Let's try it!" While many people are instinctively suspicious of change, she actually seeks it. Creators are quick to try new products and styles, and they're sometimes described as flip, spontaneous, whimsical, or without a plan. They adapt new ideas early and tend toward impatience. They are highly tolerant of risk and feel an urgency to act.

### Clues

- Responds to new discoveries with a let's-try-it attitude. A young Creator who sees a large, craggy tree might immediately think, *Let me climb it*—and then start climbing.

- Experiments with new ways to do routine tasks; might try different routes to work each day or constantly change furniture arrangements.

- Often enjoys taking risks, placing bets, or playing games of chance; might go skydiving or play blackjack for enjoyment of the game.

## Cautions and Tips

The Creator is likely to lose interest in the old just because it's not new. So she's apt to seek change for the sake of change alone. Also, it's helpful for the Creator to recognize that as she bounces among erratic priorities, her team can get confused or frustrated as they try to implement the details necessary to bring each idea to fruition.

Keep in mind that Creators often profile much like Creatives because, as leaders, neither one lets new ideas get buried in red tape. At times, both traits can and do show up in a single person, but they are in fact different attributes (although Creative is not included in this starter list). Here's a key difference: Where Creatives see revelations and patterns, then translate them into new conclusions and ideas, Creators take a chance on those ideas and move them forward. When Monet first treated light in a novel way in an oil painting, he showed a Creative attribute (one that happened to define the impressionist movement). But later, he joined with a group of fellow artists to start a new exhibition where he could display the work, thereby avoiding the established, state-sponsored jury show. In doing so, he helped pave the way for the public to see groundbreaking works sooner than previously possible—and revealed a let's-make-it-happen attitude that's indicative of a Creator.[6]

## Example

The comic-book character Iron Man is a classic Creator. (And, incidentally, he's also an example of the Creative and Creator attribute existing in the same person.) His risk tolerance is off the charts, he's obsessed with the latest technologies and toys, and he responds to new ideas by trying them out instead of analyzing potential outcomes. His spontaneity is so extreme that it's often a source of comedy, and those around him seem to worry that he doesn't have a plan.

## DECISIVE

A Decisive wants to take the wheel, make the decision, be in charge. But his desire for authority is not related to power; it's a reflection of his determination to move on and make things happen. Not only are Decisives quick to make choices, but they also don't second guess or look back. If a decision they've activated appears to be wrong, they'll change it on the fly just as quickly as they made the choice in the first place. And they don't spend (they would say "waste") time blaming themselves, circumstances, or other people. They just adjust and move forward. Decisives tend to behave as if a delayed decision is always worse than a sub-ideal decision.

## Clues

- Often comes to a decision before others on the team.
- When shown a challenge, responds with "I'll go" or "Let me take it from here" or "I'll handle it" or "Sure I can."

- Doesn't appear to doubt himself or others; tends to exhibit presence and confidence, appearing self-assured.

- Doesn't play the blame game or engage in second-guessing.

## Cautions and Tips

Many people are strongly drawn to Decisive leaders because they create high clarity. But Decisives should watch out for leaving the team in the dust, because they often don't take the time to build group ownership. Instead, they explain decisions en route, after the choice has been made.

If you're *not* highly Decisive, it's worth noting a common misconception: After watching a Decisive make a decision, it's easy to assume that he's very sharp and fast with analysis. Not necessarily. His quick conclusions don't depend on analysis but on a strong drive and ability to make decisions easily.

## Example

Ronald Reagan appeared to be a high Decisive. He chose a path, explained it simply, and made no recriminations afterward. For example, in his first year as president, Reagan made a very bold move in response to an illegal strike by the Professional Air Traffic Controllers Organization: He fired the strikers when they defied a back-to-work order. His decision left a few loyal controllers, new hires, and managerial staff in control of US skies—and threatened to ostracize one of the few labor unions that had supported his run for president. But the airways remained safe, and Reagan emerged with the reputation of a strong leader who was willing and able to make tough decisions.[7]

## DEVELOPER

If you have worked under a Developer, you likely list her as one of your best bosses (or coaches, teachers, pastors, and others). She is an encourager of people—a *yes you can* person. She delegates well, trusts others, and empowers them to act. Over time, people will open up to a Developer as a mentor because she tends to focus on others achieving goals—whether team members, colleagues, or superiors. She is self-effacing and humble, and she works behind the curtain instead of seeking the spotlight. If you mess up, a Developer will be less interested in creating a penalty and more focused on whether you learned from your mistake.

## Clues

- Encourages teamwork and enjoys coaching, teaching, or helping others grow.

- Often responds to a compliment by explaining how the team or other individuals deserve credit.

- Appeals with "I need your help" because that's what *she* likes to do: help.

- If you take her a new idea, she will either present it as yours or have you step into the spotlight yourself.

## Cautions and Tips

Developers often err on the side of keeping underperformers in a position for too long, believing that improvement will come eventually. This situation is exacerbated further if the manager is both high Developer and high Responsible (described later), in which case she will not only give the poor performer extra leeway but will also focus more on what she as a manager could have done to better help, train, or support the person—or foresee the problem before it appeared.

## Example

Robert Redford, the actor and movie director, shows a high Developer pattern. Though a hugely successful actor in his own right, he has focused a great deal on creating a launching pad for new performers and moviemakers. Redford has donated a large portion of land to his Sundance Institute, along with equipment, advice, and exposure to help support fledgling filmmakers as they get started in the industry.[8]

## LEARNER

The Learner focuses on continuous learning. He likes to mull things over and incubate ideas. He does not like being pushed to rapid conclusions. The Learner wants people to understand the context of the situation. For him, knowledge itself is the objective—rather than the end or decision to which the knowledge might lead. If you're talking to a Learner at a party and you wonder aloud about some historical question, don't be surprised when he returns an hour later with the answer, having researched the question on his smartphone right away.

## Clues

- Reviews history and background in team discussions about upcoming decisions; wants further study and analysis.

- Likely to say things like "Let's take a minute and look at the decisions that led to where we are now" or "I'll think about it" or "Let me review it first."

- Likes to know facts, history, and information as an end in itself—not necessarily to achieve a result.

- Avoids reaching the end conclusion; when faced with a decision, chooses to gather more information.

## Cautions and Tips

Learners can look to the results produced by Decisives and others for proof that time—like information—is important in the decision-making process. When seeking additional facts before taking action, a Learner should remind himself that having *all* the information is often less important than having *enough* information to move forward. Particularly in business, it's often necessary to proceed while a great deal of information is not only unknown but still unknowable as well. These are great opportunities to learn the value of judgment and intuition.

## Example

The filmmaker Stanley Kubrick was probably a Learner. He was known for his intelligence, his tendency to collect new knowledge, and his extreme perfectionism. Counterparts expected his movies to shoot for at least a year, because he would spend hours studying and analyzing only a few seconds of film at a time, seeking to define the precise tone that he wanted to communicate and the exact details that would best reflect it.[9]

## LOGICIAN

Logicians perceive the world as operating on logic. They see cause and effect: $X$ happens, therefore $Y$ result occurs. Logicians analyze numbers and graphs because they instinctively believe that the answer is in the data. Over time, they have (correctly) observed that people's feelings, senses, and emotions do not follow logical patterns, so they are suspicious of those factors. Logicians are typically introspective and serious. They think about their own behaviors and thoughts, applying the cause-effect analysis to themselves as well as others.

## Clues

- Distrusts conclusions that stem from input like "I *sense* this is the reason" or "I *feel* that she's negative toward our proposal."

- Asks "Why am I doing this?" and "Is this what I want to be doing to achieve the result?"

- Says things like "That doesn't make sense" and "It's simple logic."

- When data is shared at meetings, will stop relating to others and hone in on the charts, graphs, and figures.

## Cautions and Tips

Logicians can come across as aloof or cold-hearted, and they're often in danger of ignoring the emotional and nonlogical factors at play in people's choices. "So what," says the Logician? Well, emotions play a big role in success: Many people don't care how much a person knows until they know how much that person cares. And even ideas and products designed for logical applications will have a broader appeal when they tap into emotions.

## Example

Larry Page and Sergey Brin, cofounders of Google, both show many Logician traits. These men are clearly gifted in areas that others consider highly complex: mining huge amounts of data, analyzing patterns, and developing robust new technologies. But they have both been open about the great challenge of managing people, pointing to their need for growth in areas like emotional sensitivity and communication.[10]

## ORDERLY

An Orderly focuses on details rather than concepts. Shown an idea, her mind quickly moves to thoughts about how to actually get it done. She seeks and creates structure, and she likes things organized, in their place, and labeled. Orderlies prefer routines so that things can be done in sequence and the same way as last time. They create systems to follow up on promises they make. They appreciate precision and correctness. Especially when combined with the Logician, the Orderly can envision an organized system yielding a predictable outcome in the end.

## Clues

- Makes lists, charts, and formats to lay out a project.

- Seeks consistency, stability, and predictability.

- Generally keeps a neat office; likely to line up pad and pencil.

- May straighten pictures on the wall or circle typos in handouts distributed at meetings.

## Cautions and Tips

Orderlies have a tendency to see small issues as big problems. They can also miss the "why" completely, showing little interest in or understanding of long-term goals. When presenting to groups, Orderlies should be aware that too much detail or information can make an audience lose interest; it's a good practice to ask how much each step matters. Whenever possible, address only the three most important items.

## Example

Mary Poppins is a wonderful example of an Orderly. She values tidiness and organization, demands proper behavior, and prefers "spit spot" promptness and dress. When presented with a messy nursery, she not only seeks to create order but also immediately develops a plan (and a song) for doing so. And she clearly appreciates correctness, proudly describing herself as "practically perfect in every way."

## PERSUASIVE

A Persuasive's instinct is for closing the deal, getting the result, and achieving the objective. He is focused on winning other people to his view. He wants to convince them, convert them. He likes confrontation and is motivated by rejection. A Persuasive is in charge, commanding and guiding relationships and processes to an end result he wants to accomplish. He relates to other people in order to achieve an objective.

## Clues

- Enjoys confrontation.

- Feeds on the challenge of rejection; the word *no* lights up his competitive spirit.

• Very persistent. After appearing to give up, actually returns shortly with a new approach to convincing his audience.

## Cautions and Tips

People often say, "I'm good at sales. I must be a Persuasive." Not per this definition. Effective sales results stem from other attributes as well (Developer and Relational most notably). A Persuasive is more akin to what many would call a closer—or sometimes a pushy person.

## Example

The famous "show me the money" scene from the movie *Jerry Maguire* provides a great illustration of the Persuasive attribute in action. Cuba Gooding Jr.'s character (Rod Tidwell) is relentless in achieving his objective—namely, to ensure that his commitment to a single sports agent will be matched by that agent's dedication to securing him a lucrative contract. Despite Jerry's attempts to end the call quickly, this Persuasive character keeps him on the phone, commanding and guiding their conversation until he feels satisfied in having achieved his desired outcome. This example also reveals an often missed subtlety of the Persuasive's approach: He doesn't necessarily come up with a new pitch or enhanced argument every time he returns for another round of convincing. Often, he does just what this character does: stays the course, repeats, and wears down his listener with sheer persistence.

## RECONCILER

A Reconciler wants the people around her to get along and be happy, and she abhors conflict. She wants the team to move forward together in cooperation and tends to prioritize others' enjoyment of the work over objectives. The boss of one high Reconciler I coached once lamented to me, "Bill, it's almost like she would sacrifice performance objectives if it meant people would get along better." He was amazed and intended to exaggerate. I told him, "No, it's not *almost* as if she would; she *definitely* would. In her book, happiness among team members is more important than goals."

### Clues

- Desires consensus and often won't move forward without it.
- Continuously checks in to ensure that team members are in agreement.
- Prioritizes enjoyment, fun, and pleasure above goals.
- Will pause progress if a team member is unhappy.

### Cautions and Tips

Beware that a Reconciler may compromise objectives if it means that team members will enjoy themselves and be happy. But nonetheless, this attribute can make for excellent management in certain situations. For example, a Reconciler may be an ideal leader in a repetitive work environment where teams value the workplace social atmosphere above the content of the work itself (e.g., insurance adjusting, telemarketing, data entry, etc.). Reconcilers are also a positive force when managing people who serve the public (hotels, restaurants, etc.), because servers tend to treat customers as they themselves are treated—meaning that a Reconciler's focus on keeping teams happy can translate to happy customers.

## Example

Dorothy from *The Wizard of Oz* is a Reconciler. She so wants everyone to get along that she is actually willing to put herself in harm's way to demand accord, as when she bravely confronts the unknown lion that picks on her crew. Much of her quest reflects the Reconciler attribute: Despite the fact that Dorothy's goal is to return to Kansas, she spends most of her journey helping others pursue happiness—seeking a brain for the scarecrow, a heart for the tin man, and courage for the lion in lieu of keeping focused on her main objective.

## RELATIONAL

A Relational looks at the world in terms of how people feel. He is comfortable with the idea that human beings are illogical and operate on the basis of emotions—in fact, he expects others to do just that. When listening to people's problems or joys, a Relational's internal antennae see through the facts and tune in to feelings. He cares about others' emotional response and can be so empathetic that he actually has a physical reaction (his eyes tear up or his skin tingles). Relationals relate to others at a personal level—not to achieve an end result.

## Clues

- Cares for those who hurt.

- Seeks people who are ignored by most at group functions.

- Will listen to your description and respond with something like, "I feel like you're feeling $X$."

- Recognizes what's unique in others, often building people up about things they never saw in themselves.

## Cautions and Tips

People often jump to the conclusion that a person is Relational because he or she is likable. Don't assume that this is a valid indicator. Attraction has more to do with compatible attribute profiles than with whether one party is Relational.

## Example

Newswoman Diane Sawyer is probably Relational. When she took over the *ABC World News* anchor desk, she began making gradual changes that moved the newscast toward more emotive, people-centered reporting. She frequently focused her questions on how an issue affected audience members' lives, and her consumer features reporters began to receive more face time than many others on the team. Sawyer also kept tuned in to emotions and feelings, often describing how moved she was by an interview subject's plight or how going on-site helped her get a sense for the story.[11]

## RESPONSIBLE

A Responsible has high expectations for herself, to say the least. She has a strong sense of obligation and holds herself to a standard of doing what's promised. Her own toughest critic, a Responsible is hard on herself, mentally taking the heat no matter who messed up. For example, if you miss a deadline while under a Responsible's management, she might reprimand herself for failing to remind you a third time. A Responsible's internal conversation might sound like this: "I'm not giving enough time to my children. I'm shortchanging my husband. I'm doing less for my company than I know I can. I should be spending more time with my team members. And my house is not as clean as I want it to be!"

### Clues

- Admits wrongs after making a mistake.

- Blames self no matter who is at fault.

- Is extremely reliable and committed to meeting objectives.

- Often uses phrases like "I didn't do enough" and "I should have . . ."

- Exhibits some perfectionist characteristics.

## Cautions and Tips

This can be a stressful or burdensome attribute to live with, because the Responsible puts a lot of pressure on herself—often impossible pressure—to anticipate issues that she has no real control over. But it can also lead to great success. A Responsible will often rise to high positions because she can unquestionably be counted on. She drives herself to meet goals. And bosses, colleagues, and others often give her higher marks than she gives herself, because the Responsible always believes she could have done better.

## Example

We find an example of the Responsible attribute in the Katniss Everdeen character from Suzanne Collins's *The Hunger Games* trilogy. Katniss seems to think it's her responsibility to protect everyone around her, volunteering to fight in her sister's place, taking a lash to shield one friend from a whipping, and choosing to sacrifice her own life to save another friend during the games. And despite making more effort than anyone to literally save her world, when undesirable (and unforeseeable) outcomes ensue, Katniss blames herself for any and all problems.

• • •

You may want to earmark this chapter before reading on, because it's a good idea to regularly revisit the attributes inventory. Read it over every so often as you get to know your own attributes better.

And refer back to it as you start learning tools for recognizing and leveraging key traits in the people around you.

As we've discussed, this is a starter list, so it's both essential and abbreviated. As you begin using attributes in your life and work, you'll probably add a few more to the inventory you use personally. My own complete list contains attributes like rule abider, care giver, fun lover, introvert, intuitive, just to name a few.

However you expand your own inventory, the attributes in this starter list will be foundational. So the notes in this chapter will help you better understand how to manage or work with others effectively. But before we get into all that, and now that we have some common traits for reference, let's take a closer look at the way these attributes tend to take shape in an individual's life and work.

# CHAPTER 4

# THE GOOD, THE BAD, AND THE GREAT

If we . . . [keep] our talent alive, one day it becomes a beautiful gift, which nourishes us, makes our lives complete.

—Subroto Bagchi

In the next chapter, we'll start looking at your personal attribute profile in detail—that's the breakdown of what attributes you're strongest in, which you struggle with most, and how you rank on all the
rest. But first, let's get clear on the terminology used in describing
and ranking these traits.

Your attribute profile is not a light switch that's flipped on for
certain traits and off for others. Instead, think of it as a dimmer

that turns the light down gradually, with your strongest attributes appearing at the top and your challenges toward the bottom. Figure 4.1 describes each category and how it differs from the next.

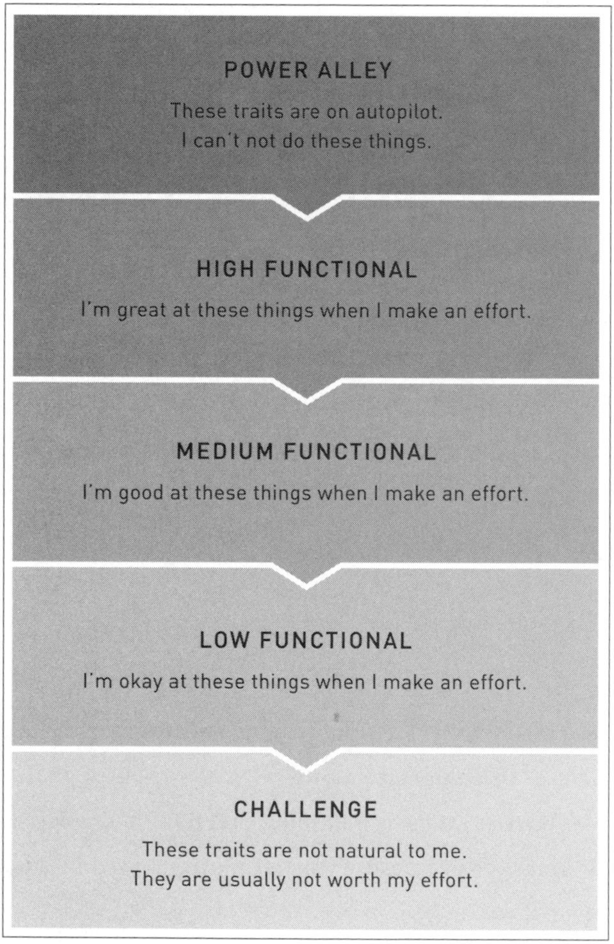

**POWER ALLEY**
These traits are on autopilot.
I can't not do these things.

**HIGH FUNCTIONAL**
I'm great at these things when I make an effort.

**MEDIUM FUNCTIONAL**
I'm good at these things when I make an effort.

**LOW FUNCTIONAL**
I'm okay at these things when I make an effort.

**CHALLENGE**
These traits are not natural to me.
They are usually not worth my effort.

**Figure 4.1**—As you create and refine an attribute profile, you will "rank" each trait according to these categories.

## POWER-ALLEY ATTRIBUTES

Power-alley attributes are the one or two attributes at the top of a person's list. Exhibiting these traits is an involuntary reaction, like blinking. They're on autopilot. One client described it like this: "My power-alley attribute just bubbles forth from me, without any effort or forethought."

In fact, it would be quite difficult (if not impossible) for a person to *avoid* demonstrating his power-alley attribute(s).

## FUNCTIONAL ATTRIBUTES

Functional attributes include any traits that don't fall into the power-alley or challenge categories. These attributes are like tools that you keep in the garage: You own them, but you don't carry them with you on your belt at all times. They're available to you, but it takes a bit of extra effort to access them.

For most people, these attributes break down further into high-, medium-, and low-functional categories, depending on how deeply they're buried in that garage. High-functional attributes are close to the power alley, but they're not actually on autopilot. Low-functional attributes are close to the challenge category, but a person can in fact exhibit them with conscious effort.

Because functional attributes are traits you can tap into with varying degrees of effort, there's a lot you can do with them to support behavior change. Again, I urge you to prioritize based on your power alley. I'll describe this through an example.

Donna had a lot of strong attributes. She was an excellent

manager, very talented at encouraging and motivating her team. And she was great face-to-face. But Donna's job had a demanding paperwork load, and more and more, it was keeping her tied to her desk in an effort to stay caught up.

Fortunately, Donna was functional in the Orderly and Responsible attributes. If she could improve upon these traits further with some effort around organization and follow up, she and her company would see a huge advantage, because she would free up more time (and brain space) for managing her team and engaging with customers—in other words, for staying focused on her power-alley gift for dealing with people. So I coached Donna on time-management skills, organizational tools, and the principles of prioritizing. I taught her a new, streamlined system for email. And she gained the knowledge and skills to remove those chains that were tying her to her desk. Her functional attributes helped her apply the new information, and in turn, her improved skills and knowledge freed her up to better leverage her greatest natural strengths.

## CHALLENGE ATTRIBUTES

Challenge attributes are the one or two attributes at the bottom of your list—the things that you just can't do well no matter how hard you work at it.

In general, I recommend that folks avoid focusing significant effort on these challenge areas, because we get so much more bang for our buck when we put energy into our natural gifts instead. In fact, in the case of challenge attributes, doing nothing is usually the best option. (It can be a real shock when you realize this, considering that you've been encouraged to work on these "issues" for most of your life.)

But there's one exception: It's worth investing some time in a challenge attribute if it gets in the way of a power-alley trait. For example, Clint was extremely strong in the Relational and Developer attributes, and—as is often the case with this combination—his sales results were stellar. His challenge attribute? Orderly. Clint was consistently late with administrative work, tended toward extreme disorganization, and operated without a calendar. This type of story is fairly common, and many companies make the mistake of threatening their Clints and implementing penalties that deflate confidence and redirect focus to the negative.

But fortunately, Clint's sales manager was smarter than that. He enlisted some outside help on Clint's paperwork but recognized that the calendar challenge would get in the way of client relationships, so we worked out an effective, attributes-savvy approach: using Clint's power alley to incentivize him.

"You are so good with customers," the manager explained. "They like you and want to see you. But if you're a no-show for appointments, you're going to disappoint them." Then, he gave Clint some practical tools and continued to work with him on his scheduling.

And it worked. By appealing to Clint's Relational trait and tapping into his associated empathy, the manager reframed the need for an accurate calendar in a way that resonated. Most essentially, the manager didn't beat Clint up over the whole spectrum of issues that came with his Orderly challenges, instead he focused on the one that threatened to dilute this great salesman's power-alley strength.

In general, you can choose to approach your own challenge attributes in different ways, depending on how much they interfere with your power-alley traits. You have a few options: You can balance them, soften them, or ignore them.

## Balancing Challenge Attributes

Balancing is the process of deliberately spending time with people who have attributes that are opposite from your own. You can learn more about opposite attribute pairings in chapter 10, but for now, let's learn by example.

Let's say I'm a natural Learner, and you're a natural Decisive. When we're in a meeting together, you confront each issue immediately, suggest a response, and are ready to move on. But I want to ponder. I ask a lot of questions and take notes. Then I open my computer and look up some things. A few minutes later, when you're already on to the next item, I return to the former topic with additional information and a few more questions.

Neither one of us is responding in the wrong way. We're responding in our own, unique ways. No matter how much I focus, I cannot make a decision on the spot and move on to the next thing immediately. And no matter how hard you try, you can't linger over a single issue, study it, explore myriad questions, and contemplate a list of potential outcomes.

But there's a middle ground: I can learn from our differences—and so can you. In fact, that's how we grow as individuals and as a team. I don't have to "fix" my weakness. I just need to recognize my challenge attributes, find and appreciate people who excel where I am less strong, learn to respect those people's input, and then turn to them when I am challenged by a situation they could help me navigate. This is the balancing process.

Here's an example. Ben had assembled an effective team of web analysts who were great at setting up analytics systems, collecting data, and delivering this information to the marketing strategy team in clear and consistent formats. The marketing folks took primary ownership of making decisions based on this data. But nonetheless, Ben noticed that his analytics team—made up primarily of high or power-alley Logicians—sometimes missed opportunities for improved collection methods or overlooked nuances within the data that might necessitate further investigation or research. The marketing folks typically recognized and requested follow-up on these items, which worked well enough. But it could work better.

Drawing on his knowledge of attributes, Ben sought out a new candidate for the analytics team—one who couldn't help but see the people behind the numbers. His hope was that this new viewpoint might help the teams avoid some extra back-and-forth, saving time and opening doors to more meaningful action. He found a high Relational who fit the bill, because she still had functional enough Logician traits to gel with the others while bringing a fresh perspective to the data. In the end, the solution was a win/win for all.

Notice that this approach does not eliminate anyone's challenge attribute. It simply helps each of us act as a sort of sandpaper on one another's rough edges. The process is tough to get used to because it means adopting a mind-set that accepts—and eventually admires—people with attributes that are opposite from our own. Instead of simply putting up with these folks, you'll actually begin seeking them out and recognizing them as great, balancing forces in your life.

## Softening Challenge Attributes

In softening a challenge attribute, you practice some parts of it, putting forth a bit of effort to become a sort of amateur practitioner. Softening is often a good approach when a challenge area is getting in the way of your power alley (as in the earlier Clint example), but it's important to begin the process by recognizing that in all likelihood, you will never make this trait a strength. Your goal here is just to soften it up—to make your challenge area a bit less challenging.

Let's say that you're a gifted Logician, but you struggle with the Relational attribute. You've been selected to lead an upcoming market study, and in many ways, you're the perfect choice for this role. But you're concerned that your challenge attribute will get in the way if you end up interviewing consumers during the research phase. So you want to soften it up a bit.

Here's the key: Be honest about what you're great at (and what you're not) when you're working to soften that challenge trait. So, since you're a Logician who prefers spending time alone in the research lab, don't force yourself to attend a speed-dating event to soften your

Relational challenges. Instead, leverage your Logician trait: Before the next company get-together, draw up a clear plan of how many people you will talk to, what questions you might ask them, and how you will remind yourself to tune in to feelings as you listen.

At first, this all might feel very strange, like you're acting a part in a poorly directed play. But don't get discouraged. Practicing a behavior—even an unnatural one—can help change your attitude about certain attributes. This fake-it-'til-you-make-it approach is often at the core of successful behavior change. And a change in attitude can be just enough to soften your challenge area and prevent it from tripping you up on the way to power-alley success.

Ann experienced this when she asked for coaching to guide her through a new challenge. She was the well-regarded top manager of a scientific research group, so it wasn't shocking that Ann was very technical, factual, data oriented, and logic focused. In our terms, a high Logician. At the same time, she was quite low in the Communicator attribute and was generally quiet and introverted. Ann enlisted my input when she got assigned to help improve communication among teams.

"Whoa! Bill, how did I get this assignment?!" she said, laughing. "And what do I do?"

We got smart: First, we designed a set of self-discovery tools for each team to use internally in smaller groups. The groups used these tools to help generate and then experiment with various ideas that might improve communication. Then, each group shared its findings with the larger team. This approach put Ann in a more comfortable position: guiding a sort of research experimentation effort—an undertaking that was right in the center of her power alley. At the same time, the participants shared results and explained their ideas for communication improvements. So Ann could direct the process effectively without communicating any more than usual (and she could learn some good communication concepts in the process!). In the end, she was able to be her natural, quiet self and guide the effort with great success.

## Ignoring Challenge Attributes

In many cases, I approach a challenge attribute with this recommendation: Ignore it. Doing so will help you focus on your strengths, and that's where the fullness of your potential lies.

It's never a bad idea to balance yourself by partnering with people on the opposite end of the attribute pool. And it certainly won't hurt to try softening those challenge areas with a bit of practice and appreciation. But eventually, you have to cut yourself some slack. Accept how you're built, appreciate who you are, and consciously let go of your challenge attributes to pursue greatness in your power alley.

• • •

With this, we've developed a strong understanding of what an attribute is, why it's important, and how it tends to act in your life and work. And we've established a starter list of many typical attributes. Now, in part II, let's apply all this to real life and start learning to identify these attributes in others and ourselves.

# IDENTIFYING

# ATTRIBUTES

# CHAPTER 5

# DETERMINING YOUR
# ATTRIBUTE PROFILE

You cannot be anything you want to be—but you can

be a whole lot more of who you already are.

—Tom Rath

In its simplest form, an attribute profile is a list of a person's attributes ranked in order of relative strength: power-alley traits at the top of the list, challenge traits at the bottom. This chapter offers a sample attribute profile, but the document itself is the easy part. The real fun lies in getting the profile nailed down and learning what to do once you have.

There are a number of steps involved in determining your profile or the profiles of the people on your team, in your family, etc. Many of these efforts are best approached through in-person consultation, but the suggestions in this chapter will provide a solid start.

## THE ATTRIBUTE QUESTIONNAIRE

Before I do an attributes seminar, I invite each participant to respond to a questionnaire. I analyze these responses to generate an initial attribute profile, and then I hand out that initial profile during the session. I always emphasize that this questionnaire is only one of several tools that can help you determine a person's attribute profile, and we'll discuss many of the others in this section.

But frankly, I've been pleasantly surprised by the ongoing accuracy of the attribute questionnaire. When I first began developing the tool many years ago, I expected to use it to create a starting point—a rough gauge of a person's attribute profile rather than a final result. But many people have found that it's right on, even after they employ all the other tools for determining and refining a profile.

For that reason, I've decided to offer this tool as a thank you to readers. Just visit www.AttributesAcademy.com to fill out your questionnaire. It should only take about twenty minutes, and your responses will generate a list of results that looks something like figure 5.1.

The letters on the left reflect where each attribute falls on our scale, listed in order from power-alley down to challenge attributes.

In this case, Ms. Volunteer is likely a power-alley Communicator and Conceptual and a high-functional Creator, Decisive, and Developer. She is medium functional from Relational through and

| RANK | ATTRIBUTES | GENERAL DESCRIPTION OF ATTRIBUTES |
|---|---|---|
| ● | Communicator | Good at writing & speaking to others. Get your point across. Inspire. Teacher. Explain well. |
| ● | Conceptual | See patterns. Strategic. Have purpose. Envision. See alternatives. Plan. Big Picture. |
| ◖ | Creator | Act on new ideas. Inspired to make change happen. Create change. Impatient. Risk tolerant. Spontaneous. Serendipitous. Act quickly. |
| ◖ | Decisive | Presence. Confidence. Self-assured. Direct decisions. Dominate. Act. "Let's try it." Want the driver's seat. |
| ◖ | Developer | Encourager. Delegator. Mentor. Focused on others achieving goals. Teamwork. Teacher. Self-effacing. Works behind curtains. |
| ◐ | Relational | Empathetic. Listens. Seeks those ignored. Cares. See people's uniqueness. Sensitivity to others' feelings. |
| ◐ | Responsible | Take the load. Feel the obligation. Do what promise. Your own toughest critic. Hard on self when you make mistake. |
| ◐ | Reconciler | Solve conflict between others. Team moves forward together. Develop consensus. Dislike conflict but not afraid of solving it. |
| ◐ | Learner | Continuous learning. Stores history. Wants to know more than do. Learning and knowledge are a worthwhile end in themselves. |
| ◐ | Achiever | Raise the bar. Measure. Keep score. Self starter. Exceed goal, then set new one. It's about improving, not beating others or impressing. |
| ◐ | Commander | Fame. Personal recognition, especially from large number of people. Enhance own control. Stature in eyes of others. Significance to others. |
| ◐ | Persuasive | Win others to your view. Command relationships. Relate to others for an end result, for moving toward objective. |
| ⊕ | Logician | Analyze. Cause & Effect. Introspective. Serious. Look for causes and logical flows of events ("of course, this caused that"). |
| ⊕ | Orderly | Detailed. Structured. Organized. Create routines. Follow up. Focus. Arrange outcomes. Precision. Consistent. Like stability. |

| KEY | | |
|---|---|---|
| | ● POWER ALLEY | ⊕ LOW FUNCTIONAL |
| | ◖ HIGH FUNCTIONAL | ⊕ CHALLENGE |
| | ◐ MEDIUM FUNCTIONAL | |

**Figure 5.1**—Sample results from an attribute questionnaire.

including Achiever, and she's probably a low-functional Commander and Persuasive. Logician and Orderly are most likely her challenge attributes. So eventually—after incorporating insights from the other tools we'll discuss in this chapter—she might end up with an attribute profile that looks similar to figure 5.2.

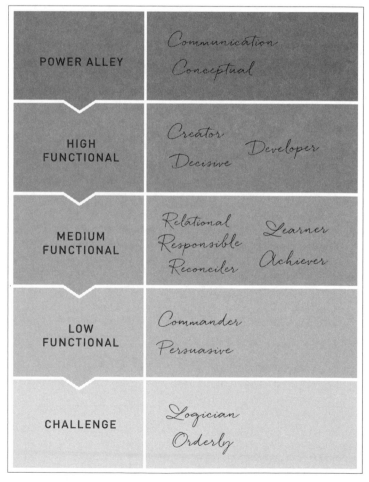

**Figure 5.2**—An attribute profile based on the results from figure 5.1.

While the questionnaire is a great starting point, I urge you to treat it as just that: a beginning. There's much more you can do to tease out and refine your (or anyone else's) profile. Let's look at some of my favorite tools now.

## EXPERIENCE ANALYSIS: THE LOVE AND DREAD LIST

To get to the heart of your attribute profile, select a trusted partner who knows you well and is willing to invest some time in your growth. This person will serve two roles: questioner and notetaker, cross examining you and recording your responses so you can focus all your energy on taking a deep dive into your past experiences.

Next, grab a fresh pad of paper and draw a vertical line down the center of several pages to create two columns. Ask your helper to write "Love" at the top of one column and "Dread" on the other—and to keep that pencil poised.

Now sit down, get comfortable, and start talking. With your love-and-dread partner asking you for details and taking thoughtful notes, discuss what you most enjoyed and disliked about kindergarten, first grade, second grade, and so on. Try to touch on all your student years—whether that extends to tenth grade or to three PhDs. Then talk about your experiences with summer camp, sports teams, church groups, summer jobs, school clubs, and volunteer activities, always focusing the conversation around what most appealed to you and repelled you. And of course, discuss your career: past jobs, projects, colleagues, vacations, and so on.

It's not important to remember all the details of each life stage.

In fact, you won't. What you will recall is the stuff that's important in determining your attribute profile. You're going for the extremes—things you loved or dreaded—which usually stick in your mind. If you don't remember much from a certain era, let it go and move on. And if you need help to get the juices flowing, you can download questions and a list template from www.AttributesAcademy.com.

At this point, chronology is less important than getting the information out of your brain and down on paper. Go ahead and jump around as things occur to you. You might be discussing junior high and blurt out, "Oh my gosh, that reminds me that I loved puzzles in kindergarten, too!" The goal is to get these realizations out of your memory and down on paper, no matter the order in which they come to you.

And always remember, this is *love* and *dread*. Not *kinda like*. We're looking for extreme feelings, not areas of gray. So your partner should stay focused on recording your strongest emotions. And he or she should be in it for the long haul, because it may take several sessions to complete your love and dread list (a good reason to pick someone you enjoy spending time with).

And speaking of partners, here's one caution as you choose the person who's going to help you walk down memory lane: As much as possible, your helper must be a catalyst but not affect the outcome. In other words, the person should take notes and probe for clarity with questions like "Is there more to say on that?" or "Do you remember more about how it made you feel?" You do not, however, want someone who says leading things, like "But you forgot to mention how much you disliked this or that." Some of the people you love most in the world might in fact make poor partners for this, so be honest when you're choosing who to invite into the process.

In my attributes seminars, I show the love and dread list in figure 5.3, and it seems to help participants understand the exercise better. This person, who was in her early thirties at the time, gave me permission to share a few pages of her list, so it's the real thing, in all its messy glory (which is why I've blocked out various names and other details for confidentiality). Take a close look. It should give you a sense of the type of memories that get shared in these sessions. If you're an astute observer, you might also notice that some issues repeat themselves throughout her life. These patterns are important, as we'll soon see.

When you've finished your love and dread list, you'll have two steps left. First, analyze the *why*. For each item on your list, make sure you've addressed the heart of what you enjoyed or detested. Say one of your loves was making oatmeal cookies with your grandmother on rainy days. *Why* did you love this? What was it about the experience that enthralled you? Did you enjoy measuring out the flour and adding the perfect amount of baking powder to make the cookies rise just right? If so, this interest could be an early sign of the Logician attribute. On the other hand, if what you most loved was spending time with your grandmother, it might point to a Relational trend.

Next, look for patterns. Once you've finished your list and fleshed out your responses by asking *why* wherever necessary, it's time to look for trends. What types of experiences seem to appear again and again in that love column? Did you always enjoy building

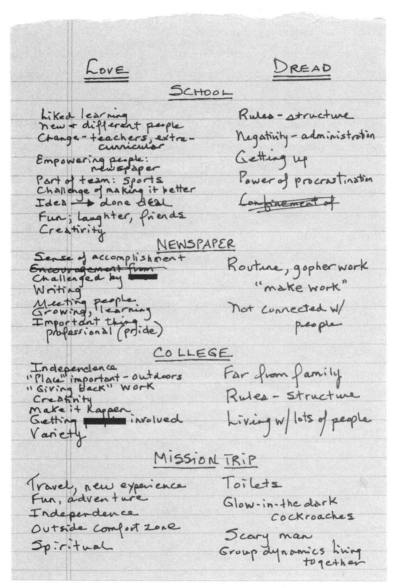

**Figure 5.3**—Example of an actual love and dread list.

things from scratch—whether blocks, products, or charity programs? If so, you might be a Creator. Have you always been big on reading, researching, and discovering new information? If yes, you're probably a strong Learner. Look for similar dread trends for insight into the attributes that elude you.

Typically, the love and dread process reveals very obvious patterns. Again and again, I hear responses like, "I can't believe I didn't see this before!" Or "I always knew I loved those memories, but I never thought about *why*." Or even, "Wow! I see that I loved high-risk adventures and experimentation all through my pre-twenty years. Now I'm so careful. What happened? Am I repressing all that?" But if the trends aren't clear to you right away, set the list down for a few days and come back to it, or ask unbiased outsiders to take a look and tell you what patterns they see.

The point of this process—and the reason it works—is that your attribute profile has been exhibiting itself throughout your life. In fact, your strongest attributes are probably natural gifts you were born with. So even if you've ended up in a role that's less aligned with your strengths, reassessing your lifelong loves and dreads should reveal the truth very quickly.

## OPPORTUNITY ANALYSIS: WHY CHOOSE YOU?

When someone offers you a new opportunity, they're also offering insight into your attribute profile. When you receive a job offer or promotion, or when you're approached to serve on a committee, there's a reason that the opportunity ended up in your lap. And that reason usually points right to your core strengths.

Take advantage of such moments to gather insight from the folks offering you the new gig. They've observed you and sensed your attributes. They've drawn conclusions, whether consciously or not. They've chosen you. Now ask them why. What traits did they see in you that were a fit with the role? This is a simple and quick question, but one that's rarely asked. And it can provide some reliable information about what you do best.

## JOY ANALYSIS: WHAT REMAINS?

Happiness changes with circumstances. But joy remains, regardless of your immediate situation. It's deeper. Even on a bad or an unhappy day, joy can stay with you.

Imagine a highly Relational woman spending a day listening to and caring for her friend Karen, who has just lost her husband, Jeff. Their conversation is long, often melancholy, and filled with hugs and tears. Later, you ask this Relational woman about her day.

"Oh, it was just great to be there with Karen at a time like this. I really felt like it helped her to talk about Jeff." She isn't *happy* about the day, but she did experience *joy* from being able to connect and help.

This phenomenon has a great deal to do with fulfillment. When you're operating in your highest attribute areas, you're more likely to experience joy, because you feel most fulfilled at these times. Knowing this can help you analyze the results of your love and dread list, and it can also help you recognize strong attributes at any time—in yourself as well as others.

What brings you that kind of satisfaction, regardless of circumstances?

## INTIMATE ANALYSIS: INPUT FROM THOSE WHO KNOW YOU BEST

You'll be amazed at how quickly your siblings, mentors, and close friends can reveal the truth about your attribute profile. Select a few whose input you respect, show them the list of attributes and definitions, and simply ask them if any of the descriptions point to you.

"Of course, this one describes you perfectly," they're likely to say. "What, you didn't know?"

It really can be that obvious to everyone around you.

Before you get started on this, take note of two cautions. First, you'll notice that I didn't mention parents in the earlier list. It's not that you can't invite your parents to participate here, of course, but the omission is intentional. While some people are blessed with genuine, adult relationships with their parents, it's rare. More commonly, parents see their children in extremes. Either they use rose-colored glasses, or they can't look at you without noting that your lowest attributes still haven't been "fixed." So be honest about your relationship with your mom or dad before you start collecting their input.

And finally, beware of the relativity trap. We see other people's attributes relative to our own. If I'm seven feet tall, a six-foot-tall person looks short. If I'm five foot six, that same person looks tall.

Likewise, a slightly organized person can seem like a power-alley Orderly to Ms. Volunteer from figure 5.1, who scored a 1 in this attribute on the basis of her answers to the questionnaire. But the same person can look far from Orderly to someone who's actually high in the trait. For this reason, it's important to know your friends and family well and keep the relativity trap in mind when considering their input.

## PASSION ANALYSIS: YOUR ENERGY AND ENGAGEMENT

If you and I became engrossed in a fascinating conversation, what would it be about? What subject could keep you energized and engaged until two o'clock in the morning?

The higher dose you have of an attribute, the more it sparks you. The lower the dose, the more it saps your vitality. So tune in to yourself. Pay attention to what gets you fired up and what gets you exhausted or drained. That's where you'll find the keys to your strongest and weakest attributes.

For example, if you can remember or plan exciting adventures until the sun comes up—say, reminisce about your latest skydive jump or plan a white-water rafting trip—your love of risk could indicate a Creator trait. If you find that an hour flies by when you sit down to write in your journal for two minutes, you might be a Communicator.

Here's another clue to the passion assessment: I constantly hear people talk about how exhausted they are at the end of the workday—or even more so, the end of the workweek. "By Friday,

I'm just fried!" These people actually feel physically tired, but is that really what their "exhaustion" is about? I suspect that much of it actually results from the mental stress of working in the basement of your attribute profile—working on the challenges rather than the power alleys.

From what I've experienced and witnessed, I can say with certainty that when a person's work reflects the top end of his attribute profile, he is energized and lit up at the end of most days. He's ignited.

Watch for these signs in yourself and in others. When you leave work feeling lit up, ask yourself what you were working on. When you're fried, ask the same question. You'll find strong clues about the top and bottom of your profile by noticing these signs.

· · ·

With all these tools in hand, you have what you need to outline your own attribute profile. As you look over the results of your questionnaire, love and dread list, and all the other tools you've chosen to use, keep in mind that—even though you see numbers in some places—this is definitely not a quantitative process. It's actually very qualitative, based on judgment, insight, and observation of patterns over time, rather than on a precise formula.

Nor is it set in stone. As you gain experience and start tuning in to others more, you might choose to raise or lower certain attributes within your own profile. That's fine. When you're ready to get your profile down on paper, you can use figure 5.2 as a guide, or format it any way you like. The look and feel is not the point. The point is to walk away with a starter profile in hand. Up until this point, you've probably spent a lot of time thinking about your own profile and gauging your own reactions to the attribute concept in general. That's a great start. Next step—expand your horizons.

In the chapters to come, we're going to turn the lens away from ourselves and start focusing on others; on how we can better understand, work with, engage, or lead the people we encounter every day. Because it's in the world outside of you that the transformative power of attributes really takes hold.

CHAPTER 6

# LISTENING [AND WATCHING] FOR REVELATION

*We don't see the world as it is; we see it as we are.*

—Anonymous

As important as it is to uncover our own attribute profiles, one of the most powerful applications of this concept actually lies in tuning in to the traits of *others*. Your boss, team members, customers, suppliers, job candidates, spouse, children, friends, peers, politicians— each one has his or her own unique attribute profile, and the better you're able to recognize and understand it, the more potential you have to optimize that relationship.

Most of us know instinctively that the better we understand a person's attributes, the better we'll be able to relate and communicate. In the end, this helps us achieve a great deal more with and through others—more of the agreement, excitement, and momentum that get teams moving forward in meaningful ways. What we don't know instinctively, however, is *how* to tune in to the many ways that people constantly reveal their own attributes. This is a learned skill and one well worth mastering.

You might be able to leverage many of the tools we discussed in the last chapter to tease out insights into others' attributes. But most often, you'll need a more, well, stealthy approach. Because let's be honest: You're not going to hand someone an attribute questionnaire during a sales call or shoulder up to a colleague at a cocktail party to take her through a love and dread list that starts with kindergarten. You need a tool you can use at the speed of life.

Only a relatively small percentage of what we can know and learn about others comes from such tools. Why? Because there's an overflowing wealth of attribute information available to us constantly, in the normal, day-to-day interactions we have. Welcome to the fine art of listening (and watching) for revelation.

## BEGINNER LISTENING: LISTENING FOR CONTENT

Fortunately, most of us have learned about the necessity of effective, active listening. This is a perennially hot topic, and rightfully so: Since most human beings are inherently focused on self (just witness the self-serving behavior of many small children as evidence), it's rarely easy or natural for us to consistently tune in to others well.

But there are a number of tools that can help us become better listeners, such as

- Focusing on others' words instead of thinking about what you'll say next
- Asking clarifying questions
- Probing to ensure that you've understood the speaker

Note that these efforts don't imply any agreement with the speaker. Rather, they show that you are tuned in—that you're paying attention and you care.

Such tools are easy to describe but challenging to adopt, so if you're still a student of these listening basics—still focused on moving from poor or mediocre listening to good listening—then I'd suggest you keep working on these building blocks while you start to practice listening for revelation. The basic skills will continue to help as you hone your advanced listening abilities.

## ADVANCED LISTENING: LISTENING FOR REVELATION

Instead of listening for content, listening (and watching) for revelation trains you to recognize what a person's words and actions reveal about their attributes—about the microchip at the core of who they are.

As you tune in to this more profound level of understanding, the person you're listening to might be oblivious to the fact that he's revealing anything. In fact, he might not even know much about his own attribute profile to begin with. But once you advance your listening skills to this level, I think you'll find that most of us are basically walking around with signs on our foreheads that read "listen and watch, and I'll tell you how I'm wired."

A client who had become a great fan of listening for revelation described it this way: He pointed out that as we were having dinner in a quiet restaurant, there were actually sounds all around us—music, news, and interviews that we couldn't hear because we didn't have a radio to tune in to those frequencies. Listening for revelation, he said, works just like this. People are constantly showing and telling us their attributes. But if we don't know how to tune in, we won't pick up a single clue.

Whether you're listening, watching, or pushing for deeper insight with probing questions, the following prompts will help you get your antennae up.

## Presuppositions

We all have presuppositions. At the outset of a conversation or experience, we make assumptions that all parties hold certain attitudes in common. If you're sitting in the home team's section at a football game, you might presume that everyone is rooting for the home team. If you move into an affluent neighborhood, your neighbors may introduce themselves and start talking property value, assuming that you're focused on financial improvement. I find that most people over sixty presuppose that I'm interested in retirement.

In much the same way, most of us have a tendency to presume

that others see the world through the lens of the traits that inspire and drive *us*. It's not a bad thing; it's just hard for many of us to imagine perspectives that we've never lived. So listen for comments like

- "Of course, everyone feels that way."
- "Obviously, that's the way most people see things."
- "Sure, I'm motivated by X—just like everyone is."

When a person assumes that "everyone" feels a certain way, he's telling you that he can't imagine *not* feeling this way. Which means that it's such an inherent part of his wiring—something he's so accustomed to seeing at work in himself—that he assumes it's a part of every life.

## Negative Reactions

We often react negatively to attributes that oppose our own. This can be extreme: "He's utterly screwed up! Otherwise, he couldn't think that." But more often, it's mild but firm:

- "Of course, John's misguided. But he still believes that the world revolves around numbers and data."
- "I get so frustrated working with Jack. He's so detail oriented. He bogs the whole group down in minutiae."
- "It drives me crazy to work with Jill. She's so focused on her 'big ideas' that we can't pin anything down."

People often react poorly to attributes that directly oppose their own. So a negative response to a certain attribute can either point to that person's challenge areas or indicate that their power alley is one that typically sits at odds with the attribute they don't like. We'll explore such "opposites" in chapter 10, but for now, note that in the previous examples, Orderly Jack and Conceptual Jill are at odds. A smart listener could see that their frustrations have to do with competing attributes, which is a great first step toward resolution.

## Seen and Unseen

When others describe an event to you, listen to the details of what they saw, how they felt, and what they think those around them felt.

I saw a great example of this when having separate conversations with two clients about their experience at a recent party. As they were mingling together, Carol saw her friend Amanda spill a glass of wine on the sofa.

"Can you imagine how awful she must have *felt?*" Carol said. "Oh, I just *hurt* for her. She must have been dying inside."

Such empathy reveals a Relational attribute. But Amanda was a Logician, so her response to the incident revealed her eye for the facts of the situation: "What'd I expect?!" Amanda laughed when I asked her about the incident later. "Of course it spilled. I was blabbing away, not looking, and I put my glass down on the edge of a book. I'm lucky I wasn't drinking red!" Carol was feeling Amanda's pain—even though it was pain that Amanda actually wasn't experiencing herself.

These were two completely different reactions to the same event, each one an indicator of the speaker's attribute.

## Best and Worst

Here's a quick way to reveal the truth about a person's attributes: Ask him about his favorite and least favorite bosses, colleagues, and so on. Then, listen for revelation rather than content, and you'll actually gain more insight into the person you're talking *to* than the person they're talking *about*. Here's a paraphrased example:

**Bill:** "Why was she your best boss ever?"

**David:** "Easy! She made me better. She set high standards all the time. She pushed me, gave me clear goals, and kept raising the bar. I loved it."

This client revealed his own Achiever attribute in describing what he appreciated about his boss. But—and this is key—note that I did not learn anything about the boss in this exchange. If that seems hard to believe, take a look at how some of David's counterparts responded to questions about the same boss:

**Karen:** "She was one of the worst managers I ever had. She only cared about the company goal, not about me improving—she was actually obsessive about the goals, so much that she didn't even notice if people were growing in their roles." Karen was a high Developer and low Achiever.

**Bob:** "I always remember her being nice to me. She liked me, I could tell. She made it obvious." Bob is high Relational.

Again, we tend to see others through the lens of our own attribute profile. So the way we describe others speaks volumes about how we're wired.

## The Magic Wand

The magic wand requires a bit more probing, but it reveals a lot. When trying to tease out attribute insights, ask this question: "If you could wave a magic wand only once and entirely fix any trait in yourself, what would it be?" The trait described will hint at the speaker's challenges.

"I'd wave the wand on my meekness. I totally avoid confrontation, and sometimes I just wish I could step up to the plate. Once, I actually worked up the nerve to ask for a promotion, but when my boss asked me why I thought I deserved it, I backed my way out of the conversation. The slightest shadow of a *no*, and I'm running for the hills. Sometimes, I wish I had it in me to push for the things I want." This response shows that Persuasive is probably a challenge trait for the individual.

But don't limit the capabilities of your magic wand. Tweak the question for more insight: "If you could wave a magic wand only once and entirely fix any issue at the company where you work, what would it be?"

"Oh, I would stop all the endless studying and analyzing and just go for it. Give new ideas a try. We'll only know if we do it!" said Will, a very high Creator.

"If you could wave a magic wand only once and entirely fix any issue in our country, what would it be?"

"I'd get together a team of the twenty smartest people I know and have them tackle one problem at a time," suggested Harrison, a power-alley Logician who laid out a detailed plan without hesitation. "Step 1, they'd state the problem. Then, analyze the causes. Finally, design a fix for each of the top three causes. Each member of the team would work alone and present his ideas to the group after outlining the proposals."

One of the great things about the wand question is that you can insert it into any conversation when someone brings up an issue she cares about.

**Her:** "I didn't like the college I attended."

**You:** "Really? Well, if you could wave a wand, how would you change things . . . ?"

Then, as always, tune in to what she shows you about herself as she responds.

## Veggies or Dessert

People enjoy working in their power alleys and dread activities on their challenge list. So to reveal attributes, it helps to get others talking about what they simply endure and what they enjoy. You can ask folks to describe their job activities as a meal: Which responsibility is the dessert? Which is the least favorite vegetable? I've heard so many memorable responses to this:

- "My dessert is watching people grow, get better, get recognized, and expand their capabilities." This man was a strong Developer.

- "I have two gross vegetables: public speaking and composing memos to large groups on big projects." Communicator was a challenge trait for this individual.

Because these questions hone in on passion and joy, you'll find that people often get very animated with their answers. If this occurs, try to remain flexible enough to stay on that subject. The goal of these questions is to tease out the things that interest the other person and then continue going further with that topic, because that's where the greatest insights lie.

## Best Praise

This is normally a reverse indicator, showing the lower end of the responder's profile—the challenge territory. Typically, people don't get excited when they're praised for their power-alley attributes, because they take these gifts for granted. They do, however, appreciate praise for lower attributes that they're working on. With this in mind, tune in to the praise that others most appreciate, as well as what they don't seem to put much stock in.

"I'd love to hear that I healed the conflicts among people around here who are at odds," Beth said when I asked her what praise she'd most like to hear. "But I avoid it. I learned early in life to just walk away." This showed that Reconciler was probably a challenge attribute for her.

"I would love to be told that I did a great job analyzing a problem and presenting the data," Robert responded when I asked him this question. His explanation revealed two attributes at once. "I'm horrible at that. Ken [his boss] is fabulous with that smart stuff. He sees conclusions I miss. And all the while, he keeps telling me I'm terrific with people. He says everyone likes me and listens to my presentations intently. So what? That's not a big deal. Ken's got the power brain. That would be great." This revealing exchange indicated Robert's high Relational attributes and his low Logician traits, because he took his most inherent gifts for granted and wished for those that he wasn't strong in just like the eagle and the loon.

## Workday Kickoff

For many of us, the beginning of the workday is a wonderful interlude: piping hot cup of coffee; quiet office; clear computer screen booting up, still uncluttered with the day's emergencies. It is in this moment, before the parade of pressing issues marches in, that we're most likely to exercise our own preferences—to do the things we most enjoy.

Tune in to how others start their day: Does Paul begin by reading an article about almost anything? He might be a Learner. Does

Sheri linger by the coffee pot catching up with colleagues? She may be Relational.

Of course, there are clear exceptions when a crisis changes our priorities. But most of the time, as we begin our day, our instincts drive us to choose dessert first and vegetables last.

## Facing Change

Others' responses to change are very revealing. So try to get your subject talking about an occasion where she was attempting to implement a change. If she never faced resistance, she probably never tried serious changes, which could be a sign of the Orderly attribute. A Creator, however, would be more likely to start his answer with something like, "Oh my gosh, there have been so many!"

Bruce, a high Persuasive and Achiever, responded to the change question with this: "When my boss gave me the project, everyone was really afraid of the change. But it didn't bother me, and the resistance from others kind of gave me a jolt of adrenaline. So I just stayed persistent and never backed down. I probably could have moved slower, but it's not my style. He gives me a goal, and I'm on it."

Melanie, a high Relational and Developer, described an obstacle that her team faced in these terms: "People just needed time to feel comfortable. They're not negative. They're just a little scared of change. So I listened, and then I listened some more. I told them I understood where they were coming from. And I *did* understand! Also, I described how the new program would help them get better and grow and do their job more effectively. Everyone liked that."

We tend to have very strong reactions to change—whether positive or negative. And it's an inevitability in our lives and careers. So this topic is fertile ground for learning about others' outlooks and attitudes.

## The Bucket List

Listen as people describe things they'd like to try or things they've done recently that were outside their comfort zone. Watch for the sparkle in their eyes while you listen.

As you tune in, keep in mind that the Creator thrives on risk, newness, and trying things out. An Orderly, on the other hand, is typically less enamored with change and experimentation. Don't forget to probe into the *why* factor here: An Achiever might dream of taking his car to a racetrack because he wants to beat the track record, while a Logician could share the same dream because it sounds fun to analyze how aerodynamics affect speed and fuel efficiency, and a Commander would hope to bathe in the limelight of the winner's circle.

Be careful not to get distracted by your own opinions about the activities others describe here. Remember, you're listening for revelation rather than content.

## What Got You Here?

Try asking your subject what got her where she is—what capabilities helped her accomplish whatever she's achieved thus far. This is a bit more straightforward than some of the other tools discussed here, but keep in mind that the world has taught most of us to focus on our deficiencies, so we're generally not accustomed to discussing such positive forces. Be patient. If the responses are slow, that's normal. Once you start teasing honest insights out, you're on track to begin revealing power-alley attributes.

For example, in an interview, Brooke told a client and me that organization and precision represented two keys to her success. When we asked her why, she thought for almost a full minute.

"Well, there are three parts to the answer," she finally began, and then she outlined a response so detailed, well supported, and specific that we saw the accuracy of her conclusion firsthand.

## Work Without Pay

Here's a great question for getting to the heart of someone's attribute profile: "If I told you that in the future, you'll have no need for money at all, but you'll still choose to do your current job, why would that be so?" Please note—this is *not* the typical "what would you do if you won the lottery" question. Far from it. You're telling people that they'll still choose to do their current job, and then you're asking them why.

Toss aside quick answers like "No way!" Encourage your subject to really think about the positive factors that could explain him doing his job for free: Creativity? The fun of being around people? An opportunity to lead? Every answer points to an attribute.

There's one other great question that will generate similar answers and insights: "If failure was impossible, what would you do?"

One of the most revealing responses to this inquiry came from a job candidate who actually rejected the question altogether. My client was looking for a risk-taking Creator. When she asked the candidate what he would do if failure were impossible, he looked confused.

"But that makes no sense. There is no such thing as 'no chance of failure.'" My client pushed a bit further, but the candidate kept avoiding any response because he thought this kind of hypothetical question was "illogical" and "didn't make sense." While my client moved on to other questions, the candidate never realized that he had revealed a very strong Logician attribute—a trait that's great in many roles, but not in the one my client was looking for.

Every answer teaches us something important.

## Team Appreciation

This team appreciation activity provides a great way to reveal attributes and build camaraderie all at once: When you have your team gathered, ask each person to share one thing she appreciates about the individual to her left. Then repeat the exercise in reverse.

Again, listen for revelation rather than information. As we've discussed, when we get people talking about others, we learn more about the speaker than the subject. The same is true in this team appreciation exercise, but the insights aren't always as black and white. Because you're specifically directing each person to share positives about a certain colleague, the responses will not always indicate similar attributes. So discern carefully and thoughtfully. Depending on how new you are to listening for revelation, you may want to jot down notes or record the session, so you can take more time to review and analyze later on.

Here's an example: Alex (a high Conceptual) once pointed out his appreciation for Samantha's (high Orderly) attention to detail. "I really depend on her to watch the specifics," he explained. "She points out important details that I don't want to think of because I don't have patience for them." In this case, Alex was valuing an attribute that opposes his own power alley.

## Good versus Best

Get a person talking about the *good* things in his life that might be crowding out time he could instead spend on the *best* things. You'll find his high-level attributes reflected in those best things. This ties back to the passion and joy that we feel when working in our power alleys.

It's very common for people to become increasingly satisfied with good things in life over time, while the best options fade from awareness. So it often takes time and a lot of questions to get a person discussing what best looks like. Here's one high-impact story I'll probably never forget.

"Bill, my vision is simple and clear," Steve began at the outset of our vision conversation. He was in his late thirties, single, and enormously successful both financially and in terms of the important position he held in the finance department of a large computer company. "I want to make as much money as I can."

"How much?" I asked.

"Oh, a hundred million. Just to be safe."

"Okay. And what would that get you?" I asked.

"What do you mean? It would get me whatever I want."

"And what do you want?" The conversation went on like this through most of dinner, with Steve describing one possession after another while I continued to ask what each would get him. It was a great, specific visioning session. And finally, after a long pause, we got to the heart of it.

"You know what it would get me? What it all would really do? It would get me back to Texas, with my brothers. Funny, that's actually all I want. They're my only family, and family's all I really care about at the end of the day."

A lot of emotion followed this discovery. And a lot of months went by before the dramatic vision change took effect. But our conversation revealed more than Steve's true life vision. It also helped us start identifying his *good* and *best* attributes.

It turns out that in his younger years, Steve had shown a staggering level of sensitivity and caring—Relational traits that he learned to suppress after many adults, including his football coach, pushed him to toughen up. Steve's ability on the field helped him secure an athletic scholarship to an excellent university, where he showed an aptitude for numbers and other typical Logician traits. So he followed a guidance counselor's advice to pursue a degree in finance. He enjoyed this type of work and learned to do it well. It was good, and Steve was perfectly fine and comfortable with good.

But when we got down to the heart of it, we discovered that his emotional connection to people, reflected in that exemplary sensitivity that had defined him so early in life, still stood at the heart of his best imaginable outcome. By learning to love good, Steve had also learned to keep his power-alley Relational attribute hidden away. That same key trait would appear again and again for Steve as our work went on, in his attribute questionnaire, love and dread list, and other tools.

## Repeated Phrases

Listen closely to the things your subject says repeatedly, because certain terms or phrases point to specific attributes. Here is a list of some typical things you're likely to hear from each attribute type:

ACHIEVER

- How much?
- How big?
- What's the highest any-
  one has gone?
- How fast could it be done?

COMMANDER

- I did this project.
- I'm conscious that every-
  one is watching me.
- My reputation is at stake.
- My goal is to . . .

## COMMUNICATOR

- Let me describe . . .
- Does this seem clear to you?
- Let's talk to her.
- Can we discuss this?

## LEARNER

- Who did what?
- How did the process work?
- What is her history?
- When was this done before?

## CONCEPTUAL

- Big picture
- Overview
- Don't get bogged down.
- It's larger than that.
- Envision this . . .

## LOGICIAN

- What caused this?
- That makes sense!
- That makes no sense!
- That's illogical.
- It's simple to explain how it happened.

## DECISIVE

- I'll go.
- Let me take it from here.
- I'll handle it.
- Sure I can.

## CREATOR

- Let's try it.
- We need to act now.
- We'll risk it.
- He's so slow!

## DEVELOPER

- Good job.
- Yes you can!
- You did that perfectly.
- What did you learn?
- I need your help with this.

## ORDERLY

- Let's put this in sequence.
- Let's organize our thoughts.
- What's our procedure?
- The devil's in the details.
- Let's dissect this further.

PERSUASIVE

- Can I get your agreement on this?
- How can I convince you?
- Let's review the benefits again.
- This can still be fixed.

RELATIONAL

- She feels so bad.
- This will upset him.
- He cares what they think.
- She must be so embarrassed.

RECONCILER

- Let's find a way to cooperate.
- Let's resolve this.
- Do you enjoy your work?
- I'm worried that will
  make people unhappy.

RESPONSIBLE

- I should have . . .
- It was my fault.
- I'll fix it.
- I know better.

Remember, everyone uses some of these phrases at one time or another. So don't jump to conclusions. What you're listening for is patterns, and once you start to notice them, you'll be amazed how much you can learn.

## WATCHING FOR REVELATION

When we talk about "listening" for revelation, we're really talking about tuning in, which involves our eyes as well as our ears. Observing people's actions can tell us at least as much about the way they're wired as listening to the words they say. When you watch Sarah react to a problem, does she search for group agreement (Reconciler), immediately step into the lead role and direct activities (Decisive),

or take the whole load on and hold herself accountable for any outcomes (Responsible)?

One caveat here—when you're watching for revelation, keep in
mind that as you consider the reasons why others behave in certain
ways, your own attribute profile can heavily bias your conclusions.
My client Debbie, a senior VP, illustrated this perfectly after an attributes session with her team. As the whole group began sharing their
thoughts about one another's attribute profiles, Debbie turned to
Lorraine, her VP of sales:

> **Debbie:** "I think your profile is accurate except for the rank-
> ing of Relational. It should be high, not low. Your customers
> love you!"

> **Lorraine:** "No, I'm low Relational. My customers don't have
> an emotional tie to me. They like me because I'm so orga-
> nized, so I follow up and make them look good."

> **Debbie:** "But you seemed personally attached to them
> during the holidays. I heard that you gave them homemade
> Christmas cookies."

> **Lorraine:** "Yeah, I made them cookies, but not because I like
> them. It was because you cut my promotional budget, and I
> couldn't buy them anything!"

After a good group laugh, they saw a great lesson: Debbie heard
the cookie story and assumed Lorraine's actions showed a Relational

attribute, but only because that's why *she herself* would have made cookies. It took tuning in further to get to Lorraine's actual motivation.

. . .

I hope you're now intrigued by the wealth of insights people around you are broadcasting throughout each day. And that you have a great selection of tools to use for tuning in to those attribute clues. We'll look at how to apply that understanding to improve relationships and productivity. But first, because practice makes perfect, let's turn to some techniques you can use to test out your listening for revelation skills, before you head for the main event.

# CHAPTER 7

# PERFECT YOUR
# LISTENING SKILLS

When you plan a journey from your mind into mine,

remember to allow for the time difference.

—Ashleigh Brilliant

I'll be honest: This listening for revelation stuff is very powerful. But, like other worthwhile things in life, it takes some effort to master. As we've discussed, one major challenge is that we don't want to be obvious about what we're doing, because discretion helps ensure that the insights we gather are as authentic as possible.

Fortunately, once you get good at listening for revelation, you won't just do it without others noticing—you'll do it without even noticing yourself, improving your understanding of the people around you with almost every conversation. But at first, it's hard to test out your skills without giving yourself away. So, while you're starting out and still rusty, you can hone your listening abilities with practice sessions that nobody else will know about.

## PRACTICE MAKES PERFECT

Mass media provides one of the greatest tools for practicing listening for revelation, letting us assess the attributes of others from afar. Here's how: Watch a television interview and practice listening for attributes rather than content. Afterward, write out your thoughts. What comments provided clues to which attributes? Be sure to keep your notes and track your impressions of various politicians, experts, journalists, and others over time. It's actually pretty fun—and very revealing.

You can do the same thing with movies. In fact, this is a great starting point. Good screenwriters develop characters that seem real. So they have attribute profiles, and their behavior and words are consistent with those profiles. Tune in, and you'll catch patterns that reveal high and low attributes. These scripted characters are a good place to start practicing your listening for revelation skills, because they're less complex than real people functioning in the real world, so they're usually easier to profile.

Here's a fun example of this method, taken from a blog post where I looked at the attributes of *Star Wars* characters.

## Yoda: Developer

Yoda shows a high Developer attribute. He's an encourager, mentor, and teacher. He facilitates teamwork and focuses on others achieving their goals, working behind the scenes to accomplish objectives.

## Princess Leia: Communicator

This brave royal shows many signs of a strong Communicator attribute. She is good at speaking with others and tends to be very effective in getting her point across. She teaches, inspires, and desires to be understood.

## C-3PO: Orderly

Detailed, organized, and consistent, C-3PO shows many characteristics of the classic Orderly. He attempts to arrange outcomes and is drawn to stability, predictability, and precision.

## Han Solo: Creator

**Princess Leia:** "What are you doing? You're not actually going into an asteroid field?"

**Han Solo:** "They'd be crazy to follow us, wouldn't they?"

**Princess Leia:** "You don't have to do this to impress me."

**C-3PO:** "Sir, the possibility of successfully navigating an asteroid field is approximately 3,720 to 1."

**Han Solo:** "Never tell me the odds!"[1]

A classic Creator quote from a great character who shows many signs of this risk-tolerant attribute. Han Solo is impatient, spontaneous, acts quickly on new ideas, and is inspired to create change. In a nutshell, he's a *let's try it* guy.

## Luke Skywalker: Learner

Luke Skywalker loves to learn. He stores history and has a strong intellectual curiosity, frequently asking questions and seeking to expand his understanding of a subject like the Force. Where Han Solo is action oriented, Skywalker is information oriented, which is typical of the Learner, who wants to *know* more than he wants to *do*.

## Chewbacca: Relational

I love this example, because it shows how much information and communication happens beyond the spoken word. Without using a language we speak, Chewie still shows a wealth of clues to his Relational trait. He listens to others, relates to them, is sensitive to their feelings, and cares for the hurt. Pure empathy, pure Relational.

• • •

Once you've tried your hand at assessing personalities from movies and the media, you can road test your listening skills at a party. Think of all those chitchatting people as attribute packages waiting to be unwrapped. The key is to take an otherwise brief, shallow inter-change and allow it to go a little deeper. So instead of this—

**You:** "Hey, how was your week?"

**Your friend:** "Ugh. Another stress-out."

**You:** "Shoot. I'm sorry. Well, you made it to Friday, anyway."

**Your friend:** "Yeah. That's at least something."

Go deeper—

**You:** "Hey, how was your week?"

**Your friend:** "Ugh. Another stress-out."

**You:** "Shoot. Why so stressful?"

**Your friend:** "Oh, my boss. She's the wicked witch."

**You:** "How's she wicked?"

**Your friend:** "Oh, not mean, nasty wicked. It's just the way she manages."

**You:** "What way is that?"

**Your friend:** "Just negative. Always finding fault. Nitpicking details."

**You:** "Which stresses you out."

**Your friend:** "Yeah. Well, it's not really stress. It's more like discouragement."

**You:** "Discouraged by her negatives?"

**Your friend:** "Yeah. Well, no. Not really. When I think about it, she was actually right about the parts I screwed up, and I knew I hadn't done my best on those. But then she didn't even mention the major things that I thought I did really great on. She just ignored the positives."

**You:** "She glossed over the good stuff and highlighted the bad, huh?"

**Your friend:** "Exactly! You know, you're right. I guess it's not so much that I've been feeling stressed as, well, hurt. I was hurt. And I know I'm sensitive—too sensitive. And she's matter-of-fact. Sometimes I'm afraid I'll get emotional and she'll think I'm acting irrationally because she's not at all that way. Actually, *that's* where the stress comes from!"

By simply engaging further, you've created a rich vein of discovery (or confirmation) about your friend the Relational. And please note—all you had to do was ask questions that rephrased what your friend was telling you. Essentially, you led her through a process of self-discovery, and in so doing, you discovered a great deal yourself.

Incidentally, notice that toward the end of this conversation (which is drawn from many real encounters I've had), your friend said you were right—even though all you'd done was rephrase her questions so she could step back and hear herself. Be prepared for this. As you stay focused on revelation, you give the other person the floor. This, in turn, allows them to verbally process their feelings. So they often come to conclusions themselves, and then credit the revelation to you. (In reality, they're not far off, because it was in fact your listening and questioning that led them to process in more depth.)

## GETTING IT RIGHT

I usually coach people through the process of learning how to listen and watch for revelation, so my clients have the distinct advantage of using me as an experienced sounding board when trying to ascertain others' areas of strength and challenge. If you're reading this book, however, you might be going it alone, so it's important to keep a few concepts in mind as you begin to hone this skill:

- Consider the anonymous quote, "We don't see the world as it is; we see it as we are." We don't see events or people through clear lenses, but rather through the screen of our own attribute structure. In recording what we see and interpret, we reveal ourselves as well as others. So please, get to know your own attributes before you embark on this journey. And always assess your interpretations of others in light of your own tendencies.

- **Don't jump to conclusions.** This process is like a game of connect the dots: After you've drawn the first few links, the big picture is still mysterious. But as you get more connections in place, the final image starts to take shape. Give it time and look for patterns rather than quick results. Most of all, remember that you can be patient with yourself: People's attributes won't go away, so they will repeatedly reveal their profiles to you. You don't need to worry about missing something in any given interchange.

Also, remember that there are two steps to all good revelation interchanges:

- **Ask and listen until you find a subject that genuinely lights up the other person—something that truly engages him or her.** Watch for bright eyes, animated gestures, and excited tones.

- **Once you find that subject, stay on the topic for as long as they show passion.** Keep asking new questions, rephrase their answers back to them for confirmation, and clarify their responses with more inquires. The longer they remain on a topic that impassions them, the more they will reveal of their attribute profile. And they're likely to learn about themselves in the process!

After all this, my final piece of advice on listening for revelation is this: Just start! The wealth of knowledge, tools, and examples we've gone over in these last two chapters might look intimidating at first. But it's really not. Again and again, clients follow up about listening for revelation within a week or two of their first attributes session, sharing comments like these:

- "Just last night, as my son reacted to a suggestion I made, I saw his Creator attribute. It came through clear as day!"

- "I've already noticed that I'm listening to my boss differently, and I'm catching stuff that's new. I understand her better already."

- "Within a few days, our sales team started discussing customers differently, recognizing attributes and brainstorming new ways to approach our relationships in light of this better understanding."

Here's the key to all these examples: People got started. They began trying out their listening skills. And within no time, they were tuned in and learning more than ever before.

• • •

But what next? Now you're tuned in and learning about the natural gifts and drivers of people around you with every exchange. The next chapter discusses how to translate all your powerful new insight into meaningful improvement in performance, engagement, and relationships in general.

# ATTRIBUTES

# IN

# ACTION

CHAPTER 8

# ATTRIBUTES AND
# PERSONAL GROWTH

I have never in my life learned anything from

any man who agreed with me.

—Dudley Field Malone

By now, you're pretty well versed in the attributes concept. You've probably gained some understanding of your own attribute profile. And hopefully, you've begun practicing the skills of listening and watching for revelation, tuning in to the many ways that those around you reveal their own attributes every day.

In parts I and II, we were in absorption mode: learning about the power of attributes and collecting insights about ourselves and others. In part III, it's time for output: How can we use this informa-tion to grow? To thrive as individuals and perform better as teams?

Fair warning—you're going to need to leave your comfort zone to do this. Because, while most of us seek comfort and are content with it, meaningful growth tends to come from some level of *discom-fort*. In the case of attributes, that healthy discomfort results from shaking up the ways we interact with others.

## VIVE LA DIFFÉRENCE

By working with and valuing people who are different from you, you can propel your personal growth—and your effectiveness in the workplace—to the next level. That's a big part of what makes this attributes concept so powerful. But everyone is susceptible to the same trap: Slowly and subtly, you surround yourself with peo-ple who show the same terrific, enjoyable, successful traits of— guess who! YOU.

As we've discussed, it's not unusual to view certain attributes as very important, others as good, and still others as relatively insignif-icant. As it relates to a specific role, this type of thinking can make a lot of sense. But if your ranking of talents aligns suspiciously well with your own attribute profile, then it's time to raise the warning flags. This is actually a major problem, because you may miss out on much of the best stuff that attributes can offer.

Let's take a couple of executives as an example: Diane and Harry. Diane is a power-alley Developer with a strong dose of Learner thrown into the mix. She encourages her team members and focuses on their growth and development. She also gathers information for a long time before acting.

Harry couldn't be more different. He is a power-alley Commander and very high Decisive. He doesn't take much personal interest in his team members, seeing them as resources that can help accomplish objectives. He also reaches conclusions quickly and makes decisions without extensive study.

With so little in common, Diane and Harry avoid working together if possible. So when they found themselves managing a major project together, it seemed like a match designed to fail. But they had both recently begun learning about and practicing these attributes concepts, so they were open minded (albeit skeptical) about approaching each other's opposing traits constructively, instead of just continuing in conflict.

As the project progressed, each became frustrated by the other's approach, as expected. However, when I asked them to list what they were *learning* from the other, both could identify clear benefits of their work together. Diane explained that she had begun to see that the group's performance sometimes suffered from her willingness to live with a team member's poor results. Her Developer tendencies meant that she continued to wait for improvement in others, often for far too long. Meanwhile, Harry admitted that he was often too quick in wanting to get rid of a team member who might be terrific in a different role.

From witnessing Harry's decisiveness in action, Diane had also learned that not all decisions require extensive information gathering. Harry, in turn, saw that he might save himself from big mistakes by toning down his quick decision trigger to make way for new information.

Notice that no one's core attribute profile changed here. However, by glimpsing the richness born of working with very different people, Harry and Diane enhanced their own individual perspectives.

## DEVELOPING THROUGH DIFFERENCES

Working with a mix of people, rather than with clones, is a powerful tool in your personal development. It constantly exposes you to the balancing effects of different attributes. At the same time, it facilitates an advanced level of collaboration, letting you focus on optimal performance in your own power-alley areas while relying on others to take on the tasks suited to their own gifts. It's an approach that's highly effective in management, and it also sets an invaluable example for your team, colleagues, and even your superiors.

Years ago, a client, Tom, did some very cool things in implementing this concept. I've since shared his approach with many others, all of whom have used it to great effect.

Tom ran a large sales and marketing team, and he had all his people attend the attributes seminar and then follow up with individual coaching sessions afterward. At the outset, he told the whole group his vision for this effort: better teamwork, less infighting, and fewer turf wars. The program was a big hit, and virtually every participant seemed open minded and excited about attributes. In a move that's typical of folks who are jazzed about a new concept, the group quickly began thinking of their own ways to integrate attributes into their day-to-day work, and they brought Tom a wonderful new idea—one that's actually pretty simple, like many great breakthroughs.

They started wearing name tags during every team meeting. But instead of putting their names on the tags, they wrote down their top two power-alley attributes and their two greatest challenge traits. After a few meetings, Tom explained that the whole atmosphere had changed—for the better. Pairs of people who had formerly been known to fight or go silent with frustration would now point to their name tags and smile. "Of course I disagree with you, Ned. I'm an Orderly and you're a Conceptual. We're *supposed* to view stuff differently. It's a good thing."

Just like that, points of contention evolved into opportunities for friendly, productive jesting. And as a result, the group began to come alive in new ways. As attributes-related terminology became part of the team's common vocabulary, they jointly began working on listening and watching for revelation with other departments. This in turn helped resolve interdepartmental spats and create opportunities for more effective communication and collaboration across teams.

Within less than a year, key leaders and team members throughout the organization were sharing stories with managers, department heads, and headquarters about how this new method of tuning in to similarities and differences was helping them get more efficient internally and realize better outcomes externally, with customers and suppliers. One day, as I rode the elevator after a follow-up coaching visit with Tom, I listened as three people I'd never coached or met discussed the attributes they'd seen at work in a meeting that morning. About a year later, Tom shared a story from a recent national meeting he'd had with all five regions, during which the president brought up the program with Tom and his four counterparts.

"I'm hearing about some new teamwork thing you're doing, Tom," he said. "Either it's really effective, or you've hired a PR agent. Whatever it is, the results are great. Don't stop."

. . .

It's true that a strong attributes program can easily make you a hero. But—as much as my coaching practice benefits from such strong company-wide results—it's the personal stories that still get me in the gut; in this case, the dozens and dozens of anecdotes about improved job satisfaction; personal breakthroughs; and repaired relationships with colleagues, family, and friends.

No matter where you apply this, as you deliberately expose yourself to different attribute structures, your own perspective will start to change in a very positive way: You'll begin to see the value of attributes in people that you used to think of as worthless—or even downright detrimental. As you grow in this more balanced view of others, you'll also see sharp improvement in the effectiveness of your people choices, team leadership, and communication with everyone from colleagues to family members.

One of the most gratifying things I hear from clients after they've absorbed the attributes concept is, "You know, this doesn't just work with my team. It works with everyone—even my teenager!"

I guess they're people too.

# CHAPTER 9

# ATTRIBUTES IN TEAMS: THE ATTRIBUTE MATRIX

Let each man pass his days in that wherein his gift is greatest.

—Propertius

If you work with or manage a team—a business unit, charitable organization, family, or any collection of people trying to pursue common goals—it is important to understand how each person's attribute profile affects him as an individual as well as how the combined profiles of all team members function as a whole. This is where the attribute matrix comes into play.

## THE ATTRIBUTE MATRIX

In essence, an attribute matrix is like an attribute profile for your entire team. It will show you what (and how many) power-alley attributes you have within the group, what challenge traits you're dealing with, and so on. It will provide visibility into the specific profiles of every person on the team and can allow for a visual representation of how attributes are distributed. In short, the matrix reveals a team's natural strengths and challenges, which in turn unearths opportunities for improved management, balance, and growth.

## CREATING A MATRIX

Start by laying out your matrix like a table. Record each person's name horizontally across the top. Then, list all attributes down the left-hand column. Ask your team members to indicate where they fall for every attribute—power, high functional, medium functional, low functional, or challenge—by entering the appropriate letter (P, H, M, L, C) in the attribute boxes below their names. Some people like to translate these "scores" into icons or colors, to give the matrix a more intuitive visual meaning, which is a great approach. Figure 9.1 shows an example of a team attribute matrix at this stage.

Ideally, you'll do this after each team member has completed his or her own personal attribute profile. But if you're working more off the cuff, keep in mind that at first, most people are unsure how to assess their strengths. This is just part of the learning curve. In fact, many people need to start working through the matrix to better

| ATTRIBUTES | BEN | LOIS | BILL | CONNIE | TERRY | PAM |
|---|---|---|---|---|---|---|
| Achiever | Power Alley | Medium Functional | Low Functional | High Functional | Medium Functional | Medium Functional |
| Commander | High Functional | Challenge | Low Functional | Power Alley | Low Functional | Medium Functional |
| Communicator | High Functional | Power Alley | Medium Functional | Medium Functional | High Functional | Medium Functional |
| Conceptual | Medium Functional | High Functional | High Functional | Low Functional | High Functional | Medium Functional |
| Creator | High Functional | Medium Functional | High Functional | High Functional | Medium Functional | Low Functional |
| Decisive | Medium Functional | High Functional | Medium Functional | Power Alley | Medium Functional | High Functional |
| Developer | Low Functional | Power Alley | High Functional | Challenge | High Functional | Medium Functional |
| Learner | Challenge | Low Functional | Low Functional | Low Functional | Medium Functional | Low Functional |
| Logician | High Functional | Medium Functional | High Functional | Low Functional | High Functional | Power Alley |
| Orderly | Low Functional | Low Functional | Low Functional | High Functional | Medium Functional | Power Alley |
| Persuasive | Power Alley | Low Functional | Low Functional | Low Functional | Low Functional | Challenge |
| Reconciler | Challenge | Low Functional | Low Functional | Challenge | Low Functional | Low Functional |
| Relational | Medium Functional | High Functional | Low Functional | Medium Functional | Low Functional | Low Functional |
| Responsible | High Functional | High Functional | High Functional | High Functional | Power Alley | Medium Functional |

KEY

- POWER ALLEY
- HIGH FUNCTIONAL
- MEDIUM FUNCTIONAL
- LOW FUNCTIONAL
- CHALLENGE

**Figure 9.1**—An example of a team attribute matrix.

assess themselves. So remind your team members that the attribute matrix is a living document that can be updated at anytime.

For example, you might initially think you're a low Communicator, but once you start working with others who clearly struggle with this attribute more than you do, you'll gain a better understanding of what low really looks like and choose to notch yourself up a bit. As folks get comfortable with the matrix, they'll grow in their ability to assess themselves, and changes will become less frequent.

If, when you create or update your matrix, you find that a team member is completely unsure of where he stands on a specific attribute, allow him to record a question mark. If this is the case, it's unlikely that the attribute in question is either extremely high or low, so it's a safe place to be a bit flexible. Moreover, I've found that by allowing people the freedom to declare "unknowns," and by leaving them the option to change their rankings in the future, you help them become more comfortable with the exercise. Additionally, you set an appropriate tone for the matrix: It's not a grade card; it's an adaptable, practical tool for moving your team forward in a positive direction.

## THE POWER OF THE MATRIX

When the matrix is complete, we can graph the results to provide a visual map of how the team profiles on various traits (see figure 9.2). You can do this on your own or by visiting www.AttributesAcademy .com for a tool that allows you to enter your team's info and receive a matrix and graph. This visual allows managers and team members

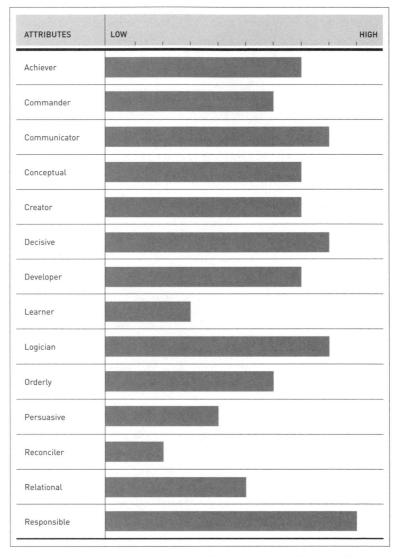

**Figure 9.2**—An example of a team's attribute mix, presented in graphic form.

quick, clear visibility into the overall group's power alleys and challenges. Which in turn creates fertile ground for learning and growth. No high Conceptuals? You might have trouble seeing the forest for the trees. A plethora of high Conceptuals? You might have a hard time getting your feet on the ground.

The matrix is also a great way to pinpoint the types of people you may need to look for when adding members to your team in the future. Perhaps you need to strengthen certain categories according to upcoming initiatives, or balance the team by bringing in opposing attributes.

It's also a helpful tool for spurring more effective action in your existing team right away. Let's say you're picking a person to handle a specific issue. Rather than selecting the team member who volunteers or seems to have the most free time, discuss what attributes would be best positioned to address the problem effectively, and pick the individual whose profile best fits the job. Similarly, the next time you're assembling a group for a specific project, you can use the attribute matrix to select members who balance one another and possess traits that will support the success of each effort.

Let's say Pete's department has a major issue and the solution centers on reconciliation. But Reconciler is one of Pete's challenges. In the past, Pete would have muddled through the process—probably without great success. But with the attribute matrix, Pete knows that Reconciler is one of Sandra's power-alley traits, so he asks her to help him. Sandra becomes Pete's internal consultant on this specific matter, and everyone wins.

. . .

As you become increasingly comfortable with the attribute matrix, you'll advance to more powerful uses for it. The information it outlines will support you in many important efforts, such as improving sales, leadership development, hiring, and so on. We'll get into all of this as we start exploring the interplay among different attribute profiles, beginning with the attributes that are most at odds.

# CHAPTER 10

# OPPOSITE ATTRIBUTE PAIRINGS

There is some good in the worst of us and some evil in the best of us.
When we discover this, we are less prone to hate our enemies.

—Martin Luther King Jr.

Some pairs of attributes typically function like opposites, meaning
that a person who is high in one tends to be low in the other. Often,
these opposing tendencies become the root of conflict among individuals with very different profiles, because we tend to underappreciate
or misunderstand people with whom we don't have much in common. But teams comprised of individuals with widely varied attributes are exceedingly powerful when managed well, that is, when
all members learn to understand and leverage one another's unique

strengths. To tap into this positive side of contrasting attributes, it's important to be aware of each trait's natural counterparts—and of the secret about successful interaction.

Let's take a closer look at some of the most common opposites.

## RELATIONAL VERSUS LOGICIAN

While the Logician sees the world in terms of rational linkages spurred by cause and effect in action, the Relational perceives events as driven by people's feelings. As these two interact with each other, it's common for frustrated thoughts to emerge.

"She's such a softie," a Logician might say of a Relational. "So worried about people's feelings that she can't see the cold, hard facts that show what we need to do. Events are controlled by cause and effect—by facts. It's a distraction and a waste of time to evaluate feelings. The data shows us the logical, rational course of action. That route may not feel good, but too bad."

Meanwhile, the Relational's response is equally impassioned: "He's so focused on numbers and facts that he can't see the people side of things, which is really the driver of our performance. He thinks we're all wrapped up in the 'soft stuff,' as he calls it. That's just his myopia! We understand that data shows one route, but that's a trap. If we ignore people's emotions, that can really scuttle our results."

## CONCEPTUAL VERSUS ORDERLY

While the Conceptual thinks of the big-picture vision from a ten-thousand-foot vantage point, the Orderly sees all the detailed steps needed to get things done down at the five-foot level. You can picture their thought processes during a meeting:

**Orderly:** "He's all big ideas, but no staying power to do the steps that'll make this stuff happen. He's going to paint this giant canvas, get everyone excited, and then it'll be a car wreck as we try to implement it and discover all the contingencies we ignored. Those surprises will grab us and drag down our momentum. The devil is in the details."

**Conceptual:** "What's the deal with all these detailed questions? She's so irritating when she tries to drag us into the mud. All this little, mundane stuff will take care of itself! The important thing is to all have the same vision. We need to be working off the same song sheet, but we don't have to sing every note the same way."

## PERSUASIVE OR COMMANDER VERSUS DEVELOPER

Both Persuasives and Commanders focus primarily on *what* gets done—the Persuasive because achieving the objective will deliver her rewards, and the Commander because achievement will enhance his image and authority. The Developer, by contrast, focuses on *how* things get done. Accomplishing goals is only part of his agenda; he's more concerned with whether the team is engaged, developing, and innovating.

Each of these folks tends to respond to success very differently:

- The Persuasive delights primarily in the promised reward.

- The Commander delights primarily in the spotlight.

- The Developer delights primarily in the growth it brings to the team or individuals.

When dealing with Persuasives and Commanders, the Developer's obstacle lies in judging them—in thinking of them as self-focused, which would carry negative connotations in the Developer's mind. And a judgmental mind-set is a huge obstacle to productive relationships.

Persuasives and Commanders run into a different challenge when managing Developers, in that they often try to motivate on the basis of personal achievement, since that's what drives *them*. But a Developer doesn't prioritize personal accomplishment in this way, so this approach is typically not effective. Meanwhile, the Persuasive or Commander is usually mystified as to why those attempts at motivation didn't work.

## LEARNER AND/OR ORDERLY VERSUS CREATOR AND/OR DECISIVE

A Learner wants to study, know facts, and check history. An Orderly wants to list, create structure, and cover the bases. In either case, the tendency is toward taking time and moving more slowly and carefully. Their perspective—"Preparation means we avoid future pitfalls. If we make sure we understand as much as we can and design the structure well in the beginning, we won't lose time fixing things in the future. Those other guys blast ahead, looking really bold and dramatic, but later, they come running to us to fix their disasters."

On the other end of the speed spectrum, the Creator is ready to try it and take the risk now, and the Decisive wants to make a choice and move ahead. Compared to our Learner and Orderly friends, these two have a completely different view of the world: "Those guys are victims of paralysis by analysis. They'd rather think than do—rather study than act. We're the ones that get the ball rolling. The future is unknowable anyway, so why prep so much? Let's get going. Then, we'll fix problems on the fly."

You can almost hear the tension in these pairings, like the ticking of a clock.

## THE SECRET TO SUCCESS

Now that you have a sense of how these opposites view the world, here's the real lesson: The attributes that are most at odds are actually the pairs that most need each other. This means that the very attribute you would naturally avoid working with is probably the one that is best suited to help you.

Relationals and Logicians can achieve mutual growth by recognizing what a great balance they are to each other. In point of fact, they're both right: The world does operate rationally, based on cause and effect—except when the power of people's feelings and perceptions pushes events in a nonrational direction. In our fast-moving world, emotions create some very extreme conditions, up to and including war. And once the extreme is the norm, people push to get some rationality back into the process. It's a teeter-totter that's been changing the world since history began.

Conceptuals and Orderlies find more balance when they learn to value their opposite's perspective. It's a highly valuable understanding, because teams need both of these attributes to optimize performance. Big-picture visions and strategies are critical to success, but more failures result from poor implementation than from poor strategy—in fact, great results can and do come from mediocre strategies that get implemented with excellence. Both sides can look at such proof as a source of humility, then avoid getting too enamored with their own viewpoints.

Developers can benefit from leaning on Persuasives and Commanders at the right times, and vice versa. Depending on the nature of the emergency, some organizational problems need the get-it-done focus of the Persuasive or Commander, regardless of *how* it's done. But for long-term viability, the Developer's approach will help grow a more sustainable team that achieves repeatable results.

When Learners and Orderlies interact with Creators and Decisives, every party can experience growth by letting the opposing attribute moderate their sense of urgency. Learners and Orderlies can observe their opposites' example and try moving faster with fewer facts where appropriate, taking action when every T is not yet crossed. At the same time, Creators and Decisives can learn how to avoid some urgency-caused crashes with a little extra prep time and forethought.

## YOUR MANTRA

In truth, a lot of this understanding is easier to describe than it is to achieve. So if you find yourself feeling negative about an attribute in another person—getting judgmental or seeing it as a "bad" trait—practice this wise mantra: *All attributes are good.*

When your colleague's attribute starts looking like bad news, whisper the mantra to yourself: *All attributes are good.* Then, follow up by thinking through why this is indeed true in your specific case.

"Okay then," you think, "what could be good about this person's approach? How can it help us? How can it assist me? How can this person help me grow?"

You can even explain your thinking to your colleague, so she can understand your appreciation for the benefits she provides and perhaps learn more about her own value. Incidentally, if you do this, she's likely to start thinking about how *your* attributes can help as well. So an added upside to this approach is that your open-mindedness and transparency can go a long way toward dissolving defensiveness in the relationship.

It might take time, but it's worth the effort.

## THE INTERPRETERS

As I noted at the outset, the attribute pairings outlined here *typically* stand in opposition to each other. But there are exceptions. Some people have a fairly high dose of both attributes in an opposite pairing. I call these individuals Interpreters.

Picture two people at opposite ends of an attribute pairing as if they're two individuals who speak different languages. They simply don't understand each other, and they have great difficulty communicating. Interpreter to the rescue. She speaks both languages, so she can help both parties better understand each other. These Interpreters are a relatively rare and valuable asset, so keep an eye out for them on your team and note which pairs of opposites they may be able to guide toward mutual understanding.

How can you identify Interpreters? They will naturally start helping opposites understand each other, describing to one what the other is trying to say. When an Interpreter joins a contentious conversation between two people with opposite attributes, you're likely to see some of these indicators:

- They'll probably show signs of understanding right away— watching and listening, using eye contact, and often nodding.

- They'll connect and communicate with both people, because they can relate to both "languages."

- You'll hear them use words like, "I hear you saying $X$" and "Do I understand correctly that you feel $Y$?"

- They will tell one person what the other means (e.g., "Mike, what I hear Rhonda saying is . . .").

If you or someone in your group tends to do this, pay attention to which attributes are involved and note the type of Interpreter you have.

It's important to clarify that when Interpreters do this, they aren't performing some extraordinarily difficult task. Interpreting is natural, just like it's natural for opposing attributes to conflict with each other—or for an eagle to fly, even though it sure looks tricky to me. And much like the eagle who doesn't seem amazed that he can soar, an Interpreter probably won't see her ability as a big deal.

• • •

With or without an Interpreter, the differences among attributes aren't just hurdles to get over. As you're sure to have learned by now, they represent myriad opportunities. They can help us find balance and achieve better outcomes. So it's worthwhile to dissect this by looking at each attribute a bit more closely in chapter 11. The more we know, the better we'll be able to work with others and manage our teams.

# STUMBLING BLOCKS AND BALANCING ACTS

I would rather be able to appreciate things I cannot have
than to have things I am not able to appreciate.

—Elbert Hubbard

As my clients get more familiar with the concept of attributes and the tools discussed in this book, they often begin to express their own desire to possess more of certain traits and less of others. This is a natural reaction, but be careful what you wish for.

I, of course, have my own unique attribute profile. But as a leadership coach, I also have the privilege of getting up close and personal with folks who are high and low in every attribute. So I can tell you that all power-alley attributes come with some baggage. The more I see, the more I recognize that each attribute is valuable and cumbersome in its own right. And there is a strong and pressing need for every one of them.

As you get to know your own profile as well as those of others, it's helpful to have some perspective on the challenges that tend to accompany each trait. This information will help you improve your own performance, balance others out, and optimize your team's potential.

## ATTRIBUTE CHALLENGES AND BALANCES

Remember our mantra: *All attributes are good.* It's completely true. But there's another side to that coin. All attributes have their benefits and their drawbacks—huge potential for great success, along with typical pitfalls. As you learn to recognize, leverage, and respond to attributes in yourself and others, you can realize great value in getting familiar with these nuances. So let's take each attribute in turn.

### Achiever

An Achiever's passion for measurement can lead her to overfocus on metrics at the expense of the intangibles at work. Relationals provide great balance here, since their tendency is to sense the emotions that can affect outcomes. Similarly, an Achiever's love of goals can lead her to an obsession with setting ever higher targets; as soon as the objective is achieved, she's raising the bar. While this can mean impressive performance, it's also important to celebrate success—if not for the Achiever, then for the team as a whole. A Developer will help encourage such pauses for celebration.

## Commander

Commanders are results-focused laser beams. They're perfect in short-term, quick-results situations—like a start-up in its early stages or an established organization that's on the brink of disaster and in need of a quick turnaround. Their challenge lies in building the organization for the long run—a task in which a Commander's opposing attribute, the Developer, tends to excel.

In general, Commanders should be aware that while they're basking in the spotlight, other contributors won't feel rewarded. But at the same time, there are plenty of people who love working in a Commander's shadow, especially in crisis—folks who want someone to take charge and move forward. For example, a Creator can find great fulfillment in working for a Commander if that boss agrees with and supports the Creator's risky bets. A Persuasive tends to be okay with the Commander taking the spotlight, because achieving the goal was all the reward she needed (and she's probably already looking to the next goal anyway).

## Communicator

Communicators tend toward lengthy meetings and emails, and they typically use lots of words and long sentences when speaking. So it's always important to check for audience interest. In conversation,

Communicators should make a conscious effort to listen, rather than focusing on what they'd like to say next. When it is time to speak, the Communicator's goal is to remember that less is more: Keep it short and simple, like Hemingway did with the written word. But keep in mind that all those extra words aren't always a bad thing. In fact, Communicators often need to process ideas and options verbally, because they tend to think better out loud. That's okay. One great approach is frankness: "I know I'm rambling, but I need to verbally process this for a minute."

## Conceptual

It's not unusual for Conceptuals to generate lots of big ideas without much action, because they're so focused on the big picture and vision that the day-to-day details needed for implementation get overlooked. One solution to this—stop disregarding the Orderly. Again and again, Conceptuals cast aside the input of Orderlies when these are the very people who can provide great support in translating big ideas into real action. Plus, by taking care of the minutiae that Conceptuals hate, the Orderly can free the Conceptual from one of her worst "vegetables"— detail—which will leave more room for her "desserts."

## Creator

Creators seek newness, which can make for fast action. But they lose interest in projects quickly and often seek change for change's sake alone. This leads to a relatively short attention span and a tendency to bounce erratically among shifting priorities and ideas.

Of course, this can be very confusing for team members, who often respond by seeking the lower-risk path of no action at all. Thus begins a problematic cycle, where the Creator sees the organization as holding her back, pushes even harder, sends up more caution flags, and slows the team even further. When this happens, it's smart for a Creator to let colleagues catch up. The Creator would also do well to look for a Communicator to partner with; since he likes to communicate and facilitate understanding, the Communicator can help slow things down until everybody gets the concept and is signed on.

## Decisive

Decisives make a choice and don't look back, which can be a powerful leadership trait. Keep in mind that other people will interpret that self-confidence and willingness to decide as competence, so many folks will assume that the Decisive knows the best course of action. The result? Others may choose not to share input that would have been quite beneficial.

My favorite approach here is complete transparency:

**Decisive:** "Let's turn right."

**Team:** Falls silent, thinking, *wow. Fifty tons of data and he just says, "Let's turn right." He must know something.*

**Decisive:** "Now, I just said that because I'm Decisive. I don't have any secret knowledge. So tell me why we should turn left—or *not* turn right."

Note that the Decisive doesn't ask his team to tell him if they disagree, which would make people less likely to speak up. Instead, his approach actually assumes that he *is* wrong.

The key here is openness and inviting input directly. Welcome others to challenge you. And seek balance from Learners, since they default to waiting, seeking more knowledge, and studying history. These two attributes have loads to learn from each other.

## Developer

Developers are wired to help, so they put a great deal of effort into others' improvement, believing that anyone can get better at anything—no matter how much evidence exists to the contrary. And if the Developer is also a Responsible, she'll feel like it's her *obligation* to manage others to success, so she's likely to invest in the wrong people for too long. If the object of the Developer's attention doesn't have the right attributes for the role, everyone's time and energy will be better served by getting that person repositioned. Commanders and Decisives can help strike the right balance here, because folks with these attributes will run out of patience with others long before the Developer.

It's also worth noting how powerful this attribute can be in sales, but in a very specific way: Because a Developer genuinely wants to help people, she needs to be truly convinced of a product, service, or idea before she can most successfully sell it to others—at which point, she'll be incredibly convincing.

## Learner

A Learner can never have enough facts, learning, history, or time to think. Since there's no limit to the amount of information he'll *want* to gather, it's important that he prioritize in advance, determining what facts he'll really *need* to move forward. Decisives and Creators can both be excellent partners in this, and the Learner can balance out these fast-moving attributes as well. But know that, like all balancing relationships, they will probably drive each other a little crazy at the outset. Try to muscle through, because these are relationships that can help all parties grow.

## Logician

Logicians tend to miss or misread the illogical, emotional factors at work in organizations, customers, suppliers, and others. Most have a strong desire to fit things into a logical formula, which can create an ongoing struggle, because the actions and reactions of human beings have a way of confounding formulas. By contrast, the reliability of numbers seems to comfort the Logician, who has a tendency to retreat into facts and figures. But numbers can appear more rational and unbiased than they actually are—a truth that's often difficult for Logicians to accept.

For balance, these folks can try giving more room to the energy and instinct of Creators and Decisives, who won't always prove a case to the Logician's satisfaction before they want to launch. Relationals will also help the Logician find balance and growth. In fact, I've seen Relationals bring Logician teammates to customer meetings, so the

Logician can watch firsthand as the customer behaves in ways they find irrational and then take note of how the Relational deals with the behavior. In many cases, the Logician sees that people are predictably unpredictable—an oxymoron that adds maturing balance to the Logician's perspective.

## Orderly

The Orderly's contribution to success is huge, because large endeavors need structure and organization. But focus on detail can reduce the Orderly's respect for the importance of vision and big-picture thinking. When losing sight of this, Orderlies do well to remember that one can do a great job getting a ladder built, strengthened, and perfectly positioned, then climb to the top rung before realizing that it's leaning against the wrong building.

Conceptuals will help keep this type of thinking front and center—which is why Conceptuals and Orderlies make powerful partners. The Orderly can also benefit from working with Creators, who are likely to prove that positive outcomes can result from serendipity, disorganization, and even chaos. When working with "messy" people like this, the Orderly can try to compartmentalize a bit, focusing on organization in his own life (briefcase, desk, car, etc.), where he has more control. By keeping most things in order and declaring a certain project, meeting room, or work relationship as the messy zone, the Orderly might find it a bit easier to put up with the disorganization around him.

## Persuasive

A Persuasive's intense focus on objectives can come across as a lack of interest in others. Well, for the most part, that's accurate. And in many cases, Persuasives who don't pretend otherwise make a good impression, because their transparency is refreshing. I once coached a high Persuasive—a really gifted closer—who told me this while his customers listened: "I don't like my customers. But I get it done for them, and they know I will. So we both win." And his customers actually laughed and nodded!

For the Persuasive, who tends to think that improving people is not the job—that it's all about the goal—the best balancing partner is the Developer, who focuses on encouragement. The Developer is also going for a goal, but by way of a different route: team achievement. Through this balancing relationship, the Persuasive might discover that he could achieve additional goals by engaging more people in his quest.

## Reconciler

Reconcilers have a tendency to sacrifice goals if it means making people happy. This can, of course, be problematic. But in work environments that require a large group of people to do routine work, Reconcilers make good managers because they create the positive social environment that's critical to keeping such teams engaged.

In general, Reconcilers should try to accept that conflict is a fact of life and work, reminding themselves that people can indeed walk arm-in-arm without seeing eye-to-eye. In other words, try to solve differences; but if you can't, get on with the goal. Persuasives and Decisives will help provide balance, because they tend to cut through conflict quickly with a "tough, let's get on with it" attitude. Although the Reconciler can't pretend to adopt this view, she will learn from the exposure.

## Relational

Relationals often have a hard time accepting or understanding facts that are not driven by emotions. They also have trouble practicing tough love or making decisions that might hurt people's feelings. Also, the Relational's time frequently gets sucked away listening to others' troubles: Someone stops by the Relational's office with a business matter, but the conversation quickly turns to a personal problem. Suddenly, the Relational is absorbed and can't turn her colleague away. One way to work through all these challenges is to partner with a very different and very balancing Logician.

## Responsible

The high Responsible holds himself to task, even for things that he doesn't have control over. Typically, the Responsible sets a very high bar, which means that he tends to achieve goals. But he can also get down on himself because of all the pressure he puts on his own shoulders.

Humor is a great tool here. It takes conscious effort, but I've seen Responsibles learn to kid themselves whenever they judge themselves harshly, and it really works to lighten things up. "Yeah right, it's my fault again! I should have anticipated this—and ended world hunger and stopped this lousy weather from coming." Laughing at yourself is a good step in accepting and forgiving yourself—which the Responsible probably needs to do often, even though he may have done nothing wrong in the first place.

Please note—a Responsible holds *himself* accountable, but he doesn't just let people walk on him. In fact, he probably has a pretty high self-image, which is why he thinks he should have anticipated the potential problem and prevented it. In many cases, this solve-it-fix-it attitude leads the Responsible to hinder other people's growth by removing consequences and alleviating adversity. A Responsible can look to Decisives or Creators for good examples of how to make mistakes and move on quickly.

## WHAT NEVER WORKS

Before we move away from this subject, I want to remind you that none of this is meant to imply that you should "overcome" your strongest attributes. Quite the opposite! Since you're wired with certain power alleys, embrace them. Know as much as you can about your attributes, try to understand how you differ from others, and optimize your best traits so you can function at the top of your potential.

In light of all this, I urge you to avoid using the phrase "you should stop being so . . ." And moreover, tune out when others use it with you. Such directives are as misguided as they are useless. So let's take a break from telling the Relational he should stop being so sensitive; from chastising the Commander for his relentless focus on getting ahead; from shaming the Creator for her impulsivity; and from correcting the Responsible with, "Stop being so hard on yourself!"

Don't stop being who you are. Start optimizing how you live.

# CHAPTER 12

# ATTRIBUTES-DRIVEN SALES AND LEADERSHIP

*The person born with a talent they are meant to use*

*will find their greatest happiness in using it.*

—Johann Wolfgang von Goethe

As you begin to understand attributes better and better, you're likely to get increasingly interested in specific tools for applying the concept in various areas of your life or business—career planning or hiring, for example. We'll explore all of these. First up is sales and leadership development, two areas where attribute concepts have wide and often very significant effect.

## IMPROVING SALES THROUGH ATTRIBUTES

Many companies have been particularly successful in leveraging the attribute matrix to enhance customer presentations, evaluate communication with prospects, and increase sales revenue. As an example, let's look at Sharon and Roger, two sales reps handling separate territories for their company. Roger was struggling with a major prospect named Larry, who had never awarded an order even though the two had enjoyed a strong rapport for three years.

I suggested that Roger seek some attribute insight from the sales team. The group discussed what they knew about the customer, and we pegged him as a high Logician. Knowing that Roger was a high Relational and low Logician—and recognizing that these are typically opposing attributes—they asked Sharon to join Larry and Roger for a lunch. Sharon was a high Logician, and her perspective might open some pathways to better results. I'll paraphrase Roger's description of the meeting.

"I introduced Sharon to Larry, and we started chatting about the industry in general. Within fifteen minutes, Larry was so engaged that I noticed ninety percent of his eye contact centering on Sharon. I excused myself and stepped outside for some phone time. I peered in a few minutes later and noticed that the two had begun diagraming something on paper. When I returned, they had sketched out an idea that Larry wanted to try. A month later, we had our first order."

Accolades to Roger! He didn't let his ego get in the way. He knew Larry *liked* him and *felt* good dealing with him, but nonetheless, something stood in the way of that order. That something was a simple matter of attribute alignment.

In this example, two people on the team made a joint sales call. But more often, sales teams leverage the attribute matrix by simply discussing certain prospects and seeking insight from colleagues who share similar attributes. Such discussions generate invaluable new insights and ideas.

But in leveraging the power of attributes to increase sales, it's not always necessary to bring a third party into the equation—nor is it always a matter of alignment. Often, with your attributes education fueling an improved understanding of what drives your customers, you can take a very direct route to more effective sales.

One client's experience with this still makes me smile every time I remember it, because it was so literal: Brent had been making proposals to Al for years. Al always invited Brent to submit a quote and would consider Brent's offers, listening carefully and asking thorough questions. But he never awarded Brent a project. After a half dozen failed attempts, Brent and I decided to evaluate their past encounters through the lens of attributes, and we discovered that Al was probably a very high Commander.

Now, Brent was a big, strong guy—a noticeable physical presence. Since Commanders want to garner attention and feel important, it seemed possible that Brent's physical size might be having a subconscious effect on Al's decision making. So I suggested he try something a bit novel.

"Why don't you find a venue where you can be physically below

Al?" I asked. "You sit while he stands—whatever works. Just try to literally position yourself below him. Also, present your bid in seconds instead of thirty minutes. Skip the drawings and details you usually use to impress him with your capability, because he might prefer to know that *he* impresses *you*."

We sketched out a sample script for Brent: "Al, I've bored you for years with charts. You know we're good at this. Today, I just bring a simple message: I need your help. You're the CEO, the sole decision maker. You can make or break my goal, and I know it. So I just ask that you award us this project to give me a chance to prove myself to you."

It took awhile for Brent to come to grips with such a different approach, but he finally figured he had nothing to lose. After all, he'd never gotten an order. So Brent organized a physical meeting place that would literally keep him looking up at Al, and he edited his message down to fifty seconds. Brent called me after the meeting, elated and amazed.

"I can't believe it," he began. "Al listened and responded almost immediately with, 'Okay, go. My operations manager has the proposal. I'll sign the papers with her this afternoon.' Then, he got up and left. It only took about a minute to get a five-million-dollar deal!"

In cases like this, communicating with attributes in mind is really about removing obstacles, so you can speak to others in a way they'll best be able to hear and understand.

## ATTRIBUTES-DRIVEN LEADERSHIP DEVELOPMENT

Now, what if you could invite others to help *you* remove such obstacles to effective communication? What if you, with your new understanding of attributes, could now use this awareness to encourage honest outside input, helping you grow as an individual and a leader? Well, you guessed it: You can.

Let's go straight to an example: Carey had long been familiar with these concepts when she sent an attribute questionnaire to everyone on her team, and to a few people from other departments with whom she interfaced frequently. She also sent it to her boss. But they weren't to fill it out for themselves; rather, she asked everyone to answer the questions in the way they thought *she* would respond.

Keeping each respondent's name confidential, we laid the answers out in a personal matrix that showed Carey's actual profile (determined beforehand) alongside the responses from others.

Before going through this exercise, we already knew that Carey was a power-alley Relational. But out of the ten total responses collected from others, only three indicated a high Relational ranking (see figure 12.1). In four cases, she actually ranked rather low for the Relational attribute. This told us that Carey's Relational power alley was not at all obvious to much of the group.

When I started asking questions about why this might be, Carey admitted that often, in office situations, she worked to withhold many of her most natural reactions because she thought her leadership role required a stern rather than sensitive hand. But at the same time, her Relational strengths had helped her rise in the company and build connected, engaged teams.

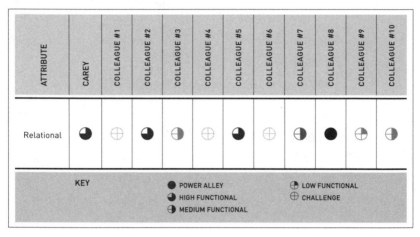

**Figure 12.1**—Carey's Relational attribute, as ranked by ten of her colleagues and herself.

So, when Carey looked at her situation in black and white, she realized that she had both a strong desire and good reasons to bring more authenticity to her workplace. And she did just that. In Carey's case, it was an easy change—she just returned to her most natural self. And shortly thereafter, she began to see a positive shift in the engagement and openness of her team.

For some people, this approach might seem a bit scary at first. But it's also fun, and it shows your team members how much you value their input and care about improving in light of it. So be a little brave, and you'll quickly uncover some of your most fruitful targets for leadership development.

We can also use attributes to help *others* grow as leaders. Greg, a higher-level executive who oversaw a number of team leaders, was great at seeing opportunities to do this, and he was very supportive of the leaders he oversaw.

One of his strongest managers, Christine, ran a department of sales technicians at a software company. Christine was a great manager and a sales dynamo herself, so her time was worth a lot to the company. But the Relational trait that helped her achieve such strong sales results also made her easy for colleagues to feel connected with, so whenever she was in the office, she'd lose large chunks of her day to people popping in to discuss their personal work or life issues. This grew to be a big problem, but at the same time—and here's the rub—her genuine caring was a major reason her highly marketable team members wanted to stay with the company.

Greg knew that he needed to redirect more of Christine's time to sales, but he also needed to keep her people engaged. So he brought in a very specific assistant for Christine: Michelle. Michelle was an extremely strong Developer, so she cared very much about helping people. Greg had Michelle's desk placed directly outside Christine's office, and he encouraged Christine to include Michelle in every meeting as well as in conversations with colleagues whenever appropriate. In this way, the assistant began building relationships with Christine's team members, connecting in a meaningful way through her genuine caring and desire to provide support, and eventually weaning much of the "counseling time" away from Christine, so she could put more effort into connecting with clients.

. . .

As we all know, no man or woman is an island. In the end, the key to doing great work is to work together in great ways. Perhaps the most foundational step in achieving such greatness lies in bringing in the right people in the first place. So in chapter 13, we'll talk about how we can apply all this to our hiring practices. It's truly a game-changing factor.

# INTERVIEWING FOR ATTRIBUTES

Human resources are like natural resources; they're

often buried deep. You have to go looking for them,

they're not just lying around on the surface.

—Ken Robinson

I am continually amazed at how little attention leaders give to the entire interviewing, selection, and hiring process—despite the fact that most companies pour boatloads of hard-earned cash into a painfully inefficient cycle of shallow interviews, gut-feel hiring, and impatient firing (or, worse, living with mediocrity).

The majority of my clients operate on an assumption that from start to finish, selection, training, termination, and rehiring costs about double the position's total salary plus benefits. And yet time and again, companies fail to streamline this giant resource suck—often because they don't make a real effort for improvement. Why get all jazzed about increasing the efficiency of your inventory system by a few percentage points, only to burn piles of comparable percentage points (and then some) with ineffective hiring practices?

If you're ready to break this cycle of waste, then it's time to talk about leveraging attributes in interviewing. One of my clients calls this "the magic trick," and I think you'll agree. Let's look at the process in two parts.

## STEP 1: GET REAL

Let's say you sell cars and I'm in the market. What am I looking for in my next vehicle, you ask? I'd like something that's small in traffic, easy to park, with good city mileage for commuting. But I want it to triple in size for those long highway trips when I need to bring lots of luggage, at which point it also needs enough power to tow my boat. But still with great fuel efficiency. Of course, in traffic jams, I want it to take off vertically and fly at a low altitude. And it should turn into a barge when necessary.

No one makes this car.

If you've listed every attribute known to man in describing your ideal candidate for a given position, then I have news for you: God didn't make this person either. He doesn't *make* people this way. He makes us unique—each with gifts, each with challenges. And just as we need to make choices when selecting a car, regardless of how much we're spending, we need to make choices when selecting the criteria for any role within our organizations.

For starters, check your role description for opposing attributes, and start to make some real decisions. Looking for someone who can help you discover, create, and evolve big-picture marketing strategies? Then you'll probably have to set aside that perennial favorite of job descriptions: "detail oriented." Want to find an analyst who's going to be fascinated by pulling substantive insights out of your streaming data? There's a good chance he's not going to also be a fast decision maker. So which is more essential to the success of the role? Choose that attribute, drop its opposite, and get results.

Your attribute matrix will come in very handy as you're working through these either-or decisions. Use it to look at your team and examine the attributes that you've got covered, as well as those where you're a bit weak. Make a list of the things you think your team needs most, and then distill it down to your three top-choice attributes. If you have trouble, ask yourself this: If your candidate was high in only three things and nonfunctional in *every other attribute* (virtually impossible), then which three would you choose? Let's bring this to life by rewriting a sample job description.

## Job Description from La-La Land

WizWiz Technology is looking for a highly motivated and experienced sales professional to manage our current customer base and create future growth. The successful candidate will have an advanced degree, preferably in computer science, and will have five to seven years of experience, showing consistent sales growth and proven client-relations success. He or she will be highly creative; will fit into our company culture without rocking the boat; will build relationships internally and externally; and will excel in providing detailed reports to our accounting department and analyzing analytics data from marketing. The role will require dramatic presentations that outline opportunities in our fast-changing technical marketplace, as well as respect for authority, acceptance and implementation of directives from management, and satisfaction with the status quo.

## Attributes-Savvy Job Description

WizWiz Technology is looking for a sales representative, and we're willing to add you to the team regardless of your degree or experience. We're mainly interested in whether your natural strengths are a fit with this role. The right candidate will either be highly tuned in to people and their emotions, very likely to encourage others and build them up, or extremely goal oriented—driven by the word "no" rather than discouraged by it. If one or two of these traits describes you, we'd like to chat, hear some examples, and have you fill out a questionnaire. One note—if you're not great at detail work, report writing, etc., don't worry. We'll find someone to help you with that.

## STEP 2: INTERVIEW FOR REVELATION

Most of us are far too easily fooled. The truth is, no candidate has it all. But in an interview, it's often hard to see who people really are, good or bad. That's why my approach works kind of like magic—because once you get it down, you hold all the cards. There's really no fooling you. You'll get straight to the truth, straight to the heart of what this person can offer your organization. And the candidates will probably feel like they simply had a nice, easy conversation—barely an interview at all. Abracadabra.

The key here is learning to listen for revelation. So when you're prepping for the interview, begin by reviewing the listening examples and prompts outlined in chapter 6. Which tactics would be appropriate for teasing out information about your target attributes? What kinds of answers would reveal the right attributes? What comments might indicate that your target traits are missing? Then, during the interview, watch and listen carefully. What topics really energize the candidate? What makes her sparkle?

This isn't about "good" answers. In fact, good answers are typically just a sign that the person says what you already believe—which may be an indication of compatible attributes, but is not necessarily a sign of the attribute for which you're interviewing. Worse yet, good can mean that the answer was clever. Nothing against cleverness, but it has little (if anything) to do with a candidate's ability to perform in a given role. Remember, we're not listening for content. We're listening for revelation—for insight into who this person is, what motivates him, and what his performance will look like if he becomes part of your team.

When you sense energy in a candidate's response to a specific question, stay on that topic. Ask follow-up questions. Once the speaker is lit up, he'll reveal more and more about his true self.

To bring this to life, let's look at an example based on an actual interview. Here, my client was looking for a manager who was a high Developer. So he asked one of the most revealing interview questions out there: Who was your worst boss ever? Then, he listened for revelation:

**Candidate:** Oh, that's easy! She was an extreme micromanager. And that drives me nuts.

**Interviewer:** What was it about the micromanaging that was such a negative?

**Candidate:** Well, it discouraged me from taking initiative, and it was kind of insulting, implying I couldn't do the job. My coworkers felt the same way. We were all afraid, just waiting to get criticized. So we all ended up stressed out, on edge.

**Interviewer:** (stays silent and keeps listening)

**Candidate:** (after a pause) But you know, even though she was hard to work for, I could have given her more feedback. We had a good relationship—she liked me. So I could have spoken to her about the micromanaging. Maybe it would have helped.

Notice how listening and probing revealed more about the candidate than what would have happened if the interviewer had just moved on after the first response. But what do these answers reveal? The candidate's awareness of her coworkers—along with her recognition that she and the boss had a good relationship—indicate a Relational attribute. One major clue is that her entire response to this question is about people's feelings rather than performance metrics. At the same time, the candidate shows clear signs of Developer and Responsible attributes when she realizes that she could have helped the manager by providing better feedback.

I think you'll quickly find that this approach to hiring will deliver richer interviews and a better sense of candidate profiles, as well as requiring you to develop higher clarity and specificity around what you're really seeking.

Also very important—you'll be conscious of what attributes you're *not* getting as well what attributes you're choosing. This mitigates eventual overreactions to "discovery" of the new person's challenge areas. The truth is, each and every one of us has our share of challenge and low attributes. Traditional approaches to interviewing give candidates myriad ways to cover these up, but by structuring your conversation around attributes and listening for revelation, you'll learn to recognize the real person—good and bad—from the outset.

. . .

Of course, all this brings up another important question: Which attributes are best suited to which roles? Let's get into those specifics now.

CHAPTER 14

# ATTRIBUTES IN DIFFERENT OCCUPATIONS

Don't ask yourself what the world needs. Ask yourself
what makes you come alive and then go do that. Because
what the world needs is people who have come alive.

—Howard Thurman

As we've learned, there are no "good" or "bad" attributes. But there certainly are attributes that fit with specific job functions. A Logician might make an excellent analyst but find a customer-service role frustrating. A Creator might be a game-changing leader in marketing but struggle in the legal department. I could go on all day. The point is, a strong attribute is only as effective as its fit with a given role.

Even in all my years of coaching, I still haven't made an exhaustive study of the occupation-attribute link, but I have observed some patterns that can help us all.

## Sales

Success in sales is strongly linked to Developer, Relational, and/or Persuasive attributes. And it's interesting to see the unique sales style typical of each. The Developer has to first convince *himself* that the offering will truly help the customer, and then he's extremely effective. The Relational focuses on building a friendship, believing that sales results will follow. The Persuasive is a closer—very focused and driven to win.

A number of other attributes support specific types of sales roles. For example, Achievers can thrive on sales teams that set strict and challenging targets, because the measurement component thrills them. High Communicators—particularly strong oral Communicators—gravitate to the presentation aspect of more complex product sales. And Responsibles are often effective in roles involving repeat sales, close tracking of inventory, and consistent customer or prospect follow-up.

## Finance and Legal

Learner, Orderly, and Logician are common to the success of financial or legal positions. This linkage makes sense because data and facts play a dominant part in such roles. In the trial attorney niche, high Communicators can flourish due to their natural ability to present issues clearly to a jury. And high Responsibles find the role of personal attorney or financial advisor a good fit, because clients can depend on them.

## Research, Development, and Engineering

Logician and Learner are common threads in these fields. The Orderly attribute also appears often in development and engineering roles where project implementation is the primary focus. But it's less apparent in research roles or in the type of development that requires a spirit of invention, because an inventor will chase dreams rather than structure. In these areas, the risk-taking nature of a Creator becomes a benefit. Also, don't overlook the unique contribution high Communicators can make in the R&D field: there's great value in a technically competent person who can explain complex (often arcane) concepts to nontechnical management from other departments.

## Manufacturing

At its core, effective manufacturing operations seek repeatability, because here, change is anathema to efficiency and quality. The more we repeat the same thing, the more efficient and accurate we become. So this field is appealing to the Orderly's focus on structure and the Logician's sense of cause and effect.

## Marketing

Conceptuals and Creators tend to be comfortable with the fact that marketing decisions are often low on precision and high on experimentation. And because they understand that consumers make decisions on the basis of feelings, sense, and "illogical" factors, Relationals are often more at ease in marketing roles than Logicians are.

In market research, a high Learner can be a precious resource. On the product development side, Conceptuals and Decisives are highly valuable—Conceptuals during initial concept development, when big-picture thinking should take precedence over detail; and Decisives toward launch time, when a willingness to pull the trigger can become essential to overcoming obstacles and moving forward.

## Customer Service

In jobs serving people, Relationals and Developers often have the best temperaments for dealing with customers on a regular basis—especially when those customers might have a complaint. And please pay close attention to the attribute profiles of the people managing your customer-service teams: The determining factor in how your reps treat your customers is how they themselves are treated. So service managers who are high Relational, Developer, or Reconciler will enhance your reps' inclination to care, help, and keep customers happy. Also, a strong Responsible attribute can be a great benefit in customer service, particularly in roles where follow-up and dependability are essential.

## Teaching

Oral Communicator and Developer are the two high attributes I most commonly observe in teachers. Relational also appears often and seems to help teachers keep tuned in to their students. And the open-mindedness and risk tolerance of the Creator attribute often enhances the impact of educators, particularly those who teach more experimental subjects like art and science.

## Medicine and Science

These fields often include many Logicians, Creators, or Commanders. Logician is no surprise, given that these fields require extensive knowledge of scientific methods and cause and effect. Creator appears most in research roles that are focused on seeking new answers and breakthroughs. And since Commanders tend to have very high confidence in their own competence, they're often well suited to surgery and the critical decision making required in the operating room.

## Entrepreneurship

Creator, Persuasive, and Commander are dominant attributes of those who thrive on taking risks, creating, or pursuing new endeavors. The Creator has a "try it" mentality and will move forward without all the facts—a helpful attitude when pursuing things that haven't been done before. The Persuasive is hyperfocused on the objective; he wants to get it done, and he's not worried about how. The Commander has the high self-confidence to depend on her own insights, which is helpful when she doesn't have a big staff to turn to for input.

In addition, Achievers often find the start-up environment a fertile arena for raising the bar, because they can compete with themselves, often with a great deal of freedom to stretch and test their own capabilities. And of course, Decisives gravitate toward the entrepreneurial world, because they like the driver's seat and will take the reins, seeking decision power and moving things forward quickly with expedient choices. With so much ground being plowed, there's rarely enough time to know all the facts before a choice must be made, so decisions often become fast and furious—a tasty proposition for this "ready, fire, aim" attribute.

## Entertainment

In most cases, entertainers have a high dose of the Commander attribute, because they seek the spotlight. In fact, they often feed on it, tapping into the energy of the audience's feedback. Relational also pops up a lot: Actors in particular exhibit this attribute, which helps them empathize with characters, emote accordingly, and sense their fellow actors to make scenes work. But musicians, singers, and composers also tend to tap into sensation and feeling, exhibiting a high dose of the Relational's empathy. Also, Reconcilers tend to thrive in the entertainment field, because they seek to create enjoyment and want to keep people happy and having fun.

Of course, considering that sports is a form of entertainment, it's worth noting here that high Achievers often make great athletes, because they love to keep score and naturally seek to be the best.

## Management and Leadership

It's generally true that folks in entry-level jobs are doers: People assessed by what they do on a day-to-day basis. Top-level jobs, on the other hand, are primarily directional: Success in these roles depends on whether the whole organization moves in the right direction over time. As an effective person moves up the ladder from doer to directional, she'll evolve into a manager—and sometimes into a true leader.

Effective managers and leaders come from all parts of the attribute spectrum. But most great leaders have a high Developer or Conceptual component. Successful short-term leaders—those who can effectively lead a company through an emergency or turnaround—typically show a lot of Persuasive and Commander traits.

•  •  •

This list should never be treated as a rigid prediction of a person's success or failure in a field. But it can help you better understand or confirm your options, and help you select strong candidates for certain roles.

Once you have the right candidate in the right role, you'll want to keep him there and help him excel. So before we close, let's look at one place where a lot of managers fall short in this regard—and talk about some ideas for doing it better.

# CHAPTER 15

# PERFORMANCE REVIEWS THAT ACTUALLY WORK

He has a right to criticize, who has a heart to help.

—William Penn

In my twenty-five years of leadership coaching, and my prior decades in management, I have heard some rendition of the following from literally hundreds of experienced managers: "Our performance review system is awful [or counterproductive, or bad, or misguided, etc.]. But inadequate as it is, we've got no idea what to do about it." Well, now you might have a solution: Incorporate attributes tools.

## THE STATUS QUO

Here's the first priority: If you grade all employees against a common list of traits, scrap this practice. This type of review system is built on the base assumption that management can declare a common attribute profile and force everyone to work toward it—regardless of whether those attributes are in a person's power alley or in the basement of their challenge traits.

But this is only the beginning of what makes the common list problematic. It's also an exercise in promoting conformity—anathema to the potential that lies waiting in the rich variety among varied people. We make better decisions when we consider dissimilar perspectives, not when we encourage people toward homogeneity. Innovation and excellence require a different approach.

But what about open-ended review systems—those not restricted to a common list of traits? In most cases, the problem with these programs is not a matter of design but rather an issue of implementation. In the vast majority of cases, open-ended performance reviews end up focused on the negative. This is likely due to our negative bias, which we addressed in chapter 2.

Whatever the cause, this negative focus does much to direct people's attention to the things they'll always struggle with, while doing almost nothing to encourage them in the ways they naturally excel. So they leave feeling defeated, deflated, and often newly obsessed with their greatest challenge attributes. Here's Jason's description of one such performance review.

"Of course my boss started with a spiel about how I'm great at people stuff, everyone likes me, I met my sales goals, yada yada. But the whole five minutes she spent on the good things, I'm thinking, *As soon as she's done with the sunshine, she's gonna drop the hammer.*"

"So, the whole time, you were *expecting* it to turn negative?" I asked.

"Sure! It always does. The rule is—pat, pat, and then whack 'em," Jason explained. "So, once she starts in on the bad stuff—on what I need to fix—that's what we talk about for the next hour. It's what this whole thing is really about: my problems."

Some managers handle performance reviews better than others, but it's a process that's inherently flawed. Why? Because performance reviews are focused on fixing negatives rather than optimizing positives.

So what to do? Use attributes, of course, starting with the following approaches.

## FROM GOOD TO GREAT

When you sit down with an eagle for a performance review, what is your goal? Do you want to get the best possible performance out of him, or the most possible conformity? Do you want to talk about how he can fly higher and farther, or do you want him to practice swimming? Most reviews send the eagle straight to the water. But if your goal is to maximize performance, then you need to make the most of this precious time. You need to get the eagle focused on soaring to new heights.

It's as simple as shifting your focus from challenge traits to power alleys—from areas of low growth potential to areas of high growth potential. As a leader, hone in on your employees' natural strengths, tell them that you're laser focused on these traits, and encourage them to adopt the same targeted determination.

Once you do this, you'll clearly see that there's nothing "soft" about this perspective. In fact, it's a very demanding approach. You're telling your people that you not only know they can be great, but you also know *how* they can be great—and so do they. So you have every expectation that they will dig into that potential at full bore, getting better and better every step of the way. Talk about high expectations.

To help us internalize this, let's imagine an example: Pretend you oversee a power-alley Reconciler who manages a customer-service team. Her reps are engaged, and customers consistently give them high marks. However, you've noticed that she's not a very decisive leader. As a Decisive yourself, this gets under your skin, and you're tempted to focus on it in her performance review. But if you do, you won't be making the best use of your time—or of this manager's talent.

Instead, how can you focus the performance review on leveraging that Reconciler trait even more? First off, tell her that you see she's a power-alley Reconciler, and you expect her to take that gift to new heights. Then, try giving her the reins on a team-building program; she's likely to excel at this. Or provide her with resources about attributes, so that she can better understand and recognize which of her team members will work well together—and who's likely to butt heads. Or, if you've found that her aversion to discord is sometimes getting in the way, you might educate her on the upside of conflict, buy her a book that explores the benefits of healthy disagreement, share stories of opposing viewpoints that have produced excellent creative outcomes, etc. In this way, you can still help her sand down some rough edges. But with an attribute-centric approach, your efforts will be much more constructive and lasting.

Now, if one of her challenge traits is actually getting in the way of her ability to excel in her power alley, then of course, you must address it. Just do so *through* her power alley, and you'll have a much better shot at spurring effective change. Let's look at how to do this.

## SPEAK TO BE HEARD

When you teach math to a five-year-old, you don't use the language of advanced calculus. You add up apples and oranges and talk about how much fruit you have.

When you offer a boat ride to someone who's never been near the water, you don't direct him to the starboard bow or ask him to drop the hook. You point toward the right side of the boat or request his help with the anchor.

If you want to tell a chef in Rome that you love her pasta, you should probably figure out how to do it in Italian.

In many situations, we instinctively know to talk to people in a language they will understand, but somehow, we keep overlooking this important factor in the context of performance reviews. This is a great first step in making your review process more impactful and effective: Stop using your own language and start thinking about the person you're speaking *to*. If you want your message to get through, you need to choose an approach that he or she can understand and absorb.

Nancy, an EVP, had reviewed Stan, one of her department managers, many times before either one knew about attributes tools. And almost every time, they spent a big chunk of their meeting talking about a negative: Stan paid lip service to his team, but he actually made little effort to develop them. He accomplished the tasks required of him and achieved quantitative goals, but he lagged severely in building his people. After discussing this issue in one performance review after another, Nancy and Stan had both become discouraged and cynical.

"In his next review," Nancy explained to me privately, "I'll talk about the problem, because I should. And he'll nod but do nothing."

Stan's attitude showed a similar sense of defeat: "She'll bring up development—for some reason, she's all about that stuff—and I'll listen and say 'Okay.' But as long as I get results and meet my goals, she'll be satisfied."

In short, Nancy and Stan had become numb to the process. When I started working with each of them on their personal attribute profiles, we discovered that Nancy was a high Developer, and Stan was a power-alley Achiever and a pretty high Commander. He was also very low in the Developer attribute, which was important here.

With this new awareness, we could now see what had been going on in their past performance reviews: Nancy was addressing Stan from the perspective of her high Developer attribute, but because this was a challenge trait for Stan, her message wasn't resonating.

She was speaking *her* language, not *Stan's* language. So, while he could hear her words, they didn't really sink in—much like an Italian-speaking chef might hear me speaking English without understanding my praise for her delicious pasta.

After seeing this, Nancy tried a new approach: talking *from* her high attribute *to* one of Stan's high attributes. Instead of talking to Stan about development as if he knew it was a priority, she changed course and spoke to his high Achiever and Commander.

"Stan, I know you're focused on reaching your team's goals, and that's great. And I have a tip for you: I think you'll find that many of your people will give you even more effort if they sense that they're also getting a chance to improve themselves in the process. So if you spend some time on developing them, you're likely to do even better versus plan. [This spoke to Stan's Achiever attribute.] Also, our company's top management, myself included, is very interested in seeing our managers encouraging others. If I can show my counterparts evidence that you're focusing on your team's growth and development, that's going to be a gold star for your personal future. [This spoke to Stan's Commander attribute.]"

Did it work? Dramatically! Within four months, Stan had set up his team's first development session in years—and with good reason, the subject was attributes! Just an aside—Nancy didn't wait until the next scheduled performance review to tell Stan he was doing a great job with this. As soon as she saw him moving in the right direction, she caught him doing it right and encouraged him to keep it up.

## THE HIGH COMES FIRST

Scolding creates defensiveness. Even if you know you're at fault, you'll probably react defensively when you feel attacked. In such situations, people are likely to look backward, focus on the problem rather than solutions, and dig their heels in, closing the window on creativity. In short, scolding is akin to pouring tar on forward progress.

"But Bill," you say, "let's be realistic. Bad things happen. Mistakes are made. And they need to be addressed. We need to find answers and learn how to avoid the same issues in the future." Of course. And ideally, we want to do this in the most effective way possible. Scolding is not it. Taking a person back to his high attributes—getting him focused on the traits that are most likely to help him find solutions, answers, etc.—usually is.

This is an approach that's essential to effective performance reviews. But it's also important at other times—usually messy times. Because this isn't about covering the world with sunshine and pat pats, making sure all your people feel swell all the time. It's about more powerful management, which includes finding smarter ways to resolve bad situations, identify failures, and move forward from mistakes. As an example, let's look at Luke's handling of a very problematic management issue.

Luke is vice president of a manufacturing services group. Valerie works for him, running global quality. She is a high Conceptual and, as is often the case with this attribute, she's not detail oriented. Valerie is also very perceptive, and she knows that she needs a high Orderly to work with her. So when she brought in Bryan, a high

Orderly who heads up a participating department, to help design a major new initiative for worldwide operations, Luke was impressed with her thoughtful choice. And the two of them did a masterful job of launching the new process.

About eighteen months later, a major problem occurred, and it led to huge costs. Root cause analysis clearly revealed that the process was still excellent and valid. But several plants hadn't followed the program properly. Nancy and Bryan's tracking had become lax, and their departments had not ensured that steps were being followed locally.

How did Luke react? A lot of us have experiences with this, wherein our managers started with something like, "What in the *world* were you thinking!? We've got a huge disaster on our hands, and it's all because you two dropped the ball."

But Luke was solution oriented. He wanted them all to learn from what went wrong and move forward quickly and effectively. So he kept Valerie and Bryan focused in their power alleys by reminding them of how to use their best attributes: "Valerie and Bryan, as I've told you before, you two did a masterful job of launching this whole global effort. You know that. You also know how serious this problem has been. So I'd like to challenge the two of you to go back to what made you great: Valerie, your vision and concepts, and Bryan, your detail and organization in implementing it. Now, you need to fix what's broken. Get back together, reignite the joint effort, and come back to me with your plan to solve this and prevent a repeat."

Luke reminded them of their top attributes, because he knew

that when they focused there, they had the best chance at success. It worked. And this time, their solution wasn't just smart at launch—it was sustainable for the long term.

· · ·

It's likely that you're already less than thrilled with your current performance-review process. So I encourage you to experiment with these attributes-based concepts. I think you'll be very happy with the results.

# CONCLUSION

Even if you are on the right track,

you'll get run over if you just sit there.

—Will Rogers

Now, dear reader, you're at a crucial split in the road.

If you choose the path on the left, you'll continue with your current way of doing things. You've probably enjoyed reading this book (or you'd have stopped by now!), and some of the concepts will occur to you now and then. You'll be glad to have this new knowledge, but it's not really going to change how you approach things.

On the right lies another path—one that will lead you to weave attributes thinking into your day-to-day existence, to realize the deep and complex power of this tool for your own life and the lives of your colleagues, team members, bosses, spouses, children, friends, and so on. As you do, you will find new richness when dealing with the world around you, and you'll probably want to begin welcoming others into the process of discovering and exploring their own attributes.

For those of you who've chosen this second path—who've decided to roll up your sleeves and dig in deeper—the first step I recommend is to begin discussing these concepts with people close to you right away: spouse, colleagues, siblings, kids, friends, superiors, and so on. It's an easy way to start processing, and it will help you expand your understanding of the concepts immediately. As we established early on, this attributes stuff tends to start making sense to people very quickly, so others are likely to jump in within minutes, applying the concept and generating specific ideas of how it fits into your story.

Next, get your free personal attribute profile. It's a great starting point—often a great overall indicator of your attributes. Just visit www.AttributesAcademy.com to get started, and to find other great resources and tools.

From there, there's a lot you can do to go further with this concept—from setting up a one-on-one coaching call to organizing a team seminar that includes individual attribute sessions. But even if you're proceeding on your own, I encourage you to practice using the many tools, prompts, and exercises outlined in this book. And whenever possible, link up with a group to discuss attributes topics on an ongoing basis and compare notes on your efforts at using them.

The point is, take action! Doing something—anything at all—is far better than doing nothing. Believe me, once you move forward, the breakthroughs you have, and the affirming feedback you get from others, will provide all the motivation you need to keep going.

And please, share your attributes stories with me. It will be an honor to know how you've taken these concepts and made them your own. I truly look forward to hearing from you. And best of luck with all your high-soaring days ahead.

# NOTES

## Chapter 1: True to Form

1. Barbara Wolff and Hananya Goodman, "The Legend of the Dull-Witted Child Who Grew Up to Be a Genius," accessed March 17, 2016, http://www.albert-einstein.org/article_handicap.html.

2. John Brownlee, "Steve Jobs's Quest for Perfection Could Make Even Buying a Sofa into a Decade-Long Ordeal," Cult of Mac, October 25, 2011, http://www.cultofmac.com/125861/steve-jobss-quest-for-perfection-could-make-even-buying-a-sofa-into-a-decade-long-ordeal/.

3. "Edison: The Wizard of Light," Teach with Movies, last updated, December 9, 2009, http://www.teachwithmovies.org/guides/edison-inventors.html.

4. Todd Pollock, "The Case for Strengths-Based Team Management," *The Jabian Journal*, Fall 2013, https://www.joomag.com/magazine/jabian-journal-fall-2013/0583318001386086091?page=78.

5. "Walt Disney: Early Failure Is Good Learning/Understanding Your Strengths and Weaknesses," Professor Nerdster blog, April 1, 2014, http://professornerdster.com/walt-disney-early-failure-good-learning-understanding-strengths-weaknesses/.

6. "The Life and Times of John Adams," U.S. History Online Textbook, accessed March 17, 2016, http://www.ushistory.org/us/19f.asp; Jack Rakove, "Sorry HBO. John Adams Wasn't That Much of a Hero," *Washington Post Opinions*, April 20, 2008, http://www.washingtonpost.com/wp-dyn/content/article/2008/04/18/AR2008041802526.html.

## Chapter 2: Our Negative Bias

1. Temple Grandin and Richard Paneck, "Temple Grandin: What's Right with the Autistic Mind," *Time*, October 7 2013, adapted from Temple Grandin and Richard Paneck, *The Autistic Mind* (New York: Houghton Mifflin Harcourt, 2013), ftp://ftp.amberton.edu/_SLatson/child%20and%20adolescent%20counseling/temple%20grandlin.pdf.

2. John Shi, "Review," *Journal of Southern History* (May 1990) 46:2 p. 336.

3. [The mystery of] ". . . his emergence from a string of catastrophic military disasters in the French and Indian War and the War for Independence with a reputation enhanced rather than ruined?" Andrew Clayton, "Learning to Be Washington," review of *Washington: A Life*, by Ron Chernow, *New York Times*, September 30, 2010; Related: Excerpt "Washington" from *Washington: A Life*, by Ron Chernow, Books of the Times, September 28, 2010.

4. "George Washington," Inside Gov, accessed March 16, 2016, http://us-presidents.insidegov.com/l/1/George-Washington.

5. Steven M. Warshawsky, "America's Greatest Presidents," American Thinker, February 20, 2006, http://www.americanthinker.com/articles/2006/02/americas_greatest_presidents.html.

6. http://www.goodreads.com/quotes/tag/mother-teresa.

7. "Grandma Moses," *Great Lives From History: The Twentieth Century*, http://salempress.com/store/pdfs/grandma_moses.pdf.

## Chapter 3: Attribute Inventory

1. Joe Morgenstern, "Worldbeater; Olympic Athlete Jackie Joyner-Kersee," *International New York Times*, July 31, 1988, http://www.nytimes.com/1988/07/31/magazine/worldbeater-olympic-athlete-jackie-joyner-kersee.html?pagewanted=all.

2. Alam Khan, "Interview: Jackie Joyner-Kersee—Beating the Odds to Be the Best of Them All," Sport 360°, November 27, 2014, http://sport360.com/article/athletics/29383/interview-jackie-joyner-kersee-beating-odds-be-best-them-all.

3. Robert Orlando, "The Foresight of Patton," *Frontpage Mag*, June 23, 2014, http://www.frontpagemag.com/fpm/234351/foresight-patton-robert-orlando.

4. Chris Isidore, "Buffett Says He's Still Paying Lower Tax Rate Than His Secretary," *CNNMoney*, March 4, 2013, http://money.cnn.com/2013/03/04/news/economy/buffett-secretary-taxes/.

5. "Seventeen of Warren Buffett's Best Quotes Analyzed," Sure Dividend, updated February 17, 2016, http://www.suredividend.com/17-of-warren-buffetts-best-quotes-analyzed/; "I never attempt to make money on the stock market. I buy on the assumption that they could close the market the next day and not reopen it for five years."

6. Beth Gersh-Nesic, "A Beginner's Guide to Impressionism," Khan Academy, accessed March 17, 2016, https://www.khanacademy.org/humanities/becoming-modern/avant-garde-france/impressionism/a/a-beginners-guide-to-impressionism.

7.  Miller Center of Public Affairs, University of Virginia, "Ronald Reagan: Domestic Affairs," accessed March 17, 2016, http://millercenter.org/ president/biography/reagan-domestic-affairs.

8.  "Independent Film," Wikipedia, last modified March 22, 2016, https:// en.wikipedia.org/wiki/Independent_film.

9.  Michael Herr, "Kubrick," *Vanity Fair*, April 21, 2010, http://www. vanityfair.com/hollywood/2010/04/kubrick-199908; Tom Cruise, Annette Insdorf, and Terry Semel, "Stanley Kubrick," *Interview*, October 22, 2012, http://www.interviewmagazine.com/film/ stanley-kubrick#_.

10. Sergey Brin and Larry Page, "Interview: Making the World's Information Accessible," *Academy of Achievement*, October 28, 2000, retrieved April 12, 2014, http://www.achievement.org/autodoc/page/pagoint-1.

11. Howard Kurtz, "After Six Months as Anchor, Diane Sawyer Is Bringing a Sharper Edge to ABC's 'World News.'" *The Washington Post*, June 28, 2010, accessed June 2014, http://www.washingtonpost.com/wp-dyn/ content/article/2010/06/27/AR2010062703064.html; J. Max Robins, "The 'Disneyfication' of ABC World News with Diane Sawyer," *Forbes*, January 10, 2014, accessed June 2014, http://www.forbes.com/sites/ maxrobins/2014/01/10/the-disneyfication-of-abc-world-news-with-diane-sawyer/#6560cbc02312.

## Chapter 7: Perfect Your Listening Skills

1.  Lawrence Kasdan and Leigh Brackett, from a short story by George Lucas, *The Empire Strikes Back*, The Internet Movie Script Database (IMSDb), accessed March 16, 2016, http://www.imsdb.com/scripts/ Star-Wars-The-Empire-Strikes-Back.html.

# ABOUT THE AUTHORS

**Bill Munn** helps leaders manage teams to their greatest potential, providing customized leadership coaching to maximize the performance of each individual. Through strategic visioning and in-the-moment issue resolution, he motivates executives, nonprofit directors, and leaders of every stripe to spur mission-driven growth.

A management-coaching veteran of twenty-six years and former top-level executive of a Dow 30 and Fortune 500 company, Bill brings real-world experience to his seminars, training programs, and one-on-one coaching, supporting hundreds of corporate leaders worldwide with practical wisdom, real-world action tools, and unbiased insight.

An MBA and former university teacher, Bill is a dynamic public speaker, an engaging blogger with a dedicated audience, and the author of two books, including *Lead or Be Led: A Guide for Intentional Living*. His online home is www.billmunncoaching.com.

Bill and his wife, Lindy, split their time between Ohio and beautiful northern Michigan, where they often welcome their three daughters, three sons-in-law, and ten grandchildren into their empty nest.

• • •

**Libby Cortez** is a power-alley Communicator who has followed her gift to a career in writing, marketing, and content magic. She and her agile little company have spent the past fifteen years supporting small businesses, sole proprietors, startups, ministries, and (yes) large organizations by bringing stories and messages to the world in smart, meaningful ways. Armed with a master's degree in creative writing from Northwestern University and a PhD in taking-action-and-learning-always from the university of real business & life, she's become a pencil-wielding crusader for the unrelenting power of the written word. Libby blogs about communication, connection, the entrepreneurial life, and more at www.libbycortez.com.

With the other twenty-six hours in each day, she joins her husband, Casey, in chasing their three small children around their hometown of Austin, Texas.